FOUNDATIONS

READING

EXPLORER

THIRD EDITION

BECKY TARVER-CHASE

DAVID BOHLKE

**NATIONAL
GEOGRAPHIC**
L E A R N I N G

Australia · Brazil · Mexico · Singapore · United Kingdom · United States

National Geographic Learning,
a Cengage Company

**Reading Explorer Foundations
Third Edition**

Becky Tarver-Chase and David Bohlke

Publisher: Andrew Robinson

Executive Editor: Sean Bermingham

Senior Development Editor: Christopher Street

Director of Global Marketing: Ian Martin

Heads of Regional Marketing:

Charlotte Ellis (Europe, Middle East and Africa)

Kiel Hamm (Asia)

Irina Pereyra (Latin America)

Product Marketing Manager: Tracy Bailie

Senior Production Controller: Tan Jin Hock

Associate Media Researcher: Jeffrey Millies

Art Director: Brenda Carmichael

Operations Support: Hayley Chwazik-Gee

Manufacturing Planner: Mary Beth Hennebury

Composition: MPS North America LLC

For permission to use material from this text or product,
submit all requests online at **cengage.com/permissions**
Further permissions questions can be emailed to
permissionrequest@cengage.com

Student Book with Online Workbook:
ISBN-13: 978-0-357-12472-7

Student Book:
ISBN-13: 978-0-357-11628-9

National Geographic Learning
20 Channel Center Street
Boston, MA 02210
USA

Locate your local office at **international.cengage.com/region**

Visit National Geographic Learning online at **ELTNGL.com**
Visit our corporate website at **www.cengage.com**

Printed in China
Print Number: 01 Print Year: 2019

CONTENTS

SCOPE AND SEQUENCE

UNIT	THEME	READING	VIDEO
1	Mysteries	**A:** A Mysterious Visitor **B:** The Lost City of Atlantis	Moon Mystery
2	Eating Extremes	**A:** The World of Speed Eating **B:** The Hottest Chilies	Science of Taste
3	Cool Jobs	**A:** Digging for the Past **B:** Getting the Shot	Right Dog for the Job
4	Shipwrecks	**A:** I've Found the Titanic! **B:** My Descent to the Titanic	An Ancient Shipwreck
5	Science Investigators	**A:** The Disease Detective **B:** At the Scene of a Crime	The Flu Virus
6	Plants and Trees	**A:** Planting for the Planet **B:** Fatal Attraction	Giants of the Forest
7	Mind's Eye	**A:** Understanding Dreams **B:** Seeing the Impossible	Parasomnia
8	Animal Wonders	**A:** A Penguin's Year **B:** Do Animals Laugh?	Amazing Narwhals
9	Building Beauty	**A:** A Love Poem in Stone **B:** The Great Dome of Florence	Brunelleschi's Dome
10	Forces of Nature	**A:** Wild Weather **B:** When Weird Weather Strikes	Tornado Terror
11	Giants of the Past	**A:** The Mammoth's Tale **B:** Monsters of the Deep	Ichthyosaurs
12	Technology	**A:** The Robots are Coming! **B:** How Will We Live in 2045?	A Social Robot

ACADEMIC SKILLS

READING SKILL	VOCABULARY BUILDING	CRITICAL THINKING
A: Scanning B: Skimming	A: Word usage: *pass* and *past* B: Word forms of *sink* and *strike*	A: Applying Ideas B: Synthesizing Information
A: Identifying the Parts of a Passage B: Pronoun Reference	A: Collocations with *argue* B: Collocations with *painful*	A: Justifying Opinions B: Applying Ideas
A: Dealing with New Vocabulary (1)—Using a Dictionary B: Understanding Suffixes	A: Collocations with *get* B: Word forms of *pay, cost,* and *spend*	A: Evaluating Advice B: Personalizing; Synthesizing Information
A: Identifying a Paragraph's Main Idea B: Recognizing Compound Subjects and Objects	A: Word usage: *agree* B: Synonyms for *totally*	A: Evaluating Arguments B: Evaluating Ideas; Justifying Ideas
A: Identifying the Purpose of a Paragraph B: Inferring Meaning	A: Suffix *-ous* B: Word forms of *possible*	A: Applying Ideas B: Evaluating Evidence; Sythesizing Information
A: Creating a Timeline of Events B: Understanding a Process	A: Word forms with *-ation* B: Collocations with *difference*	A: Justifying Opinions B: Applying Ideas
A: Organizing Information (1)—Creating a Concept Map B: Understanding Conjunctions	A: Adjectives with *-ed* and *-ing* B: Collocations with *mistake*	B: Reflecting; Applying Ideas
A: Dealing with New Vocabulary (2)—Using Context B: Identifying Supporting Details	A: Word usage: *on (your) own* B: Adjectives to describe emotions	A: Categorizing Information B: Evaluating Supporting Details
A: Annotating Text B: Understanding Infographics	A: Collocations with *promise* B: Words acting as nouns and verbs	A: Understanding Opinions B: Synthesizing Information; Inferring Information
A: Understanding Tenses B: Understanding Cause and Effect	A: Prefix *fore-* B: Synonyms and antonyms for *unusual*	A: Personalizing B: Ranking Advice
A: Understanding Passive Sentences B: Organizing Information (2)—A Chart	A: Collocations with *in* B: Suffix *-ward*	A: Discussing Pros and Cons B: Ranking
A: Identifying Examples B: Understanding Prefixes	A: Collocations with *daily* B: Word usage: *pick up*	A: Justifying Opinions B: Rating Predictions; Evaluating Ideas

READING EXPLORER brings the world to your classroom.

With *Reading Explorer* you learn about real people and places, experience the world, and explore topics that matter.

What you'll see in the Third Edition:

Real-world stories give you a better understanding of the world and your place in it.

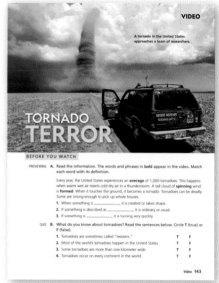

National Geographic Videos expand on the unit topic and give you a chance to apply your language skills.

Reading Skill and **Reading Comprehension** sections provide the tools you need to become an effective reader.

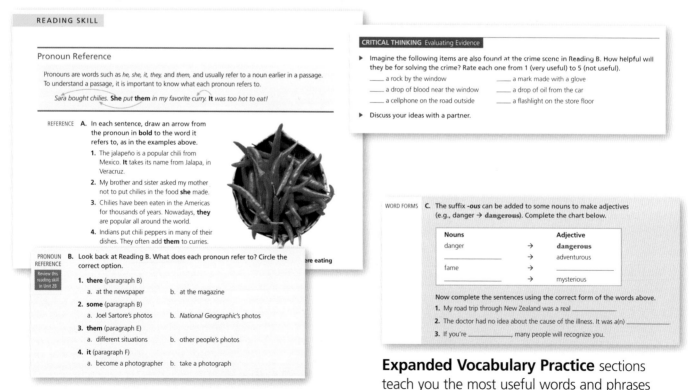

Expanded Vocabulary Practice sections teach you the most useful words and phrases needed for academic reading.

MYSTERIES

California's "sailing stones" were once a mystery. We now know that the rocks are moved by strong winds when the ground is icy.

WARM UP

Discuss these questions with a partner.

1. Read the caption. How do the rocks move?

2. Do you think there are things that science cannot explain? If so, give an example.

1A

> ⌄ An artist's drawing of 'Oumuamua—a strangely shaped object that passed by Earth. **Astronomers** are not sure if it was an **asteroid**, or something else altogether.

A MYSTERIOUS VISITOR

A   In October 2017, astronomers in Hawaii saw something surprising. A **strange** object was moving through the solar system. They had seen many asteroids before, but this was something different. It was long and **thin**—like a cucumber. The object's **speed** and direction also showed something surprising. This was an interstellar[1] object—the first ever seen.

B   The object was named 'Oumuamua—Hawaiian for "visitor from afar." Nobody is sure exactly what it is. The simplest idea is that 'Oumuamua is a strangely shaped piece of rock. Perhaps it was **knocked** out of a far-off star system. However, astronomers saw that its speed increased after **passing** the sun. Some scientists therefore suggest a different theory.

C   "'Oumuamua could be a piece of alien **technology**," says Professor Abraham Loeb from Harvard University. Loeb believes this could explain the object's long, thin shape, and also its change in speed. **Maybe** 'Oumuamua was a spaceship that came to **explore** our solar system. "All possibilities should be considered," says Loeb.

> Professor Abraham Loeb suggested that 'Oumuamua could be an alien spaceship.

D   'Oumuamua can no longer be seen from Earth. But astronomers continue to study the information they got from it. It is still not clear if the object was a large rock, or something else altogether. 'Oumuamua will likely be a mystery for many years to come.

---

1 If an object is described as **interstellar**, it has traveled between different stars.

'Oumuamua: What We Know

- Entered the inner solar system in August 2017 **❶**. Possibly came from a star system **25 light years** from our sun—a **600,000-year** journey.

- Reached a top speed of **315,800 km/h**—more than **250** times the speed of sound—as it passed the sun **❷**.

- First seen by astronomers in October 2017 when it was **33,000,000 km** from Earth—about **85** times further than our moon **❸**.

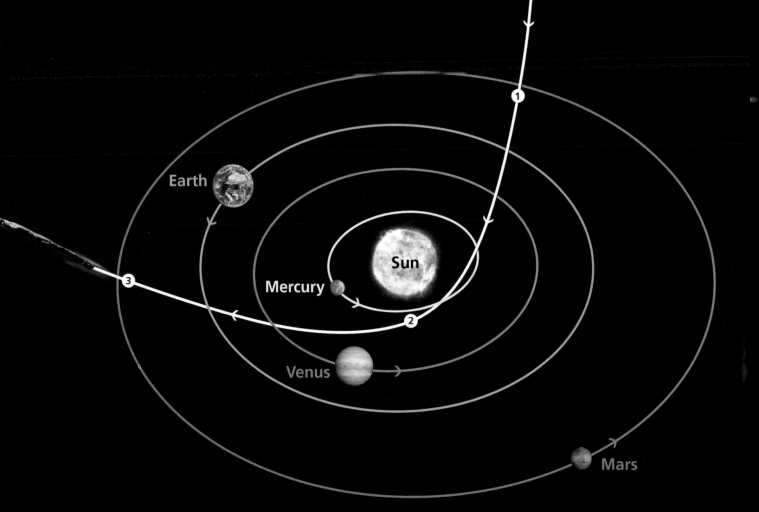

A. Choose the best answer for each question.

GIST

1. What is the reading mainly about?

a. new technology to help scientists find asteroids

b. the largest asteroid ever seen by scientists

c. a mysterious object that passed by Earth

DETAIL

2. What did scientists learn from studying 'Oumuamua's speed and direction?

a. It came from another star system.

b. It was possible it could hit the Earth.

c. It was an asteroid.

DETAIL

3. What is NOT given as a reason why 'Oumuamua could be an alien spaceship?

a. the object's size and shape

b. the object's change in speed

c. the object's color

VOCABULARY

4. In paragraph C, what does *considered* mean?

a. explained in detail

b. thought about carefully

c. chosen from a list

INFERENCE

5. According to the infographic on page 10, when was 'Oumuamua first seen from Earth?

a. as it entered the inner solar system

b. just before it passed the sun

c. after it passed the sun

Scientists believe 'Oumuamua is spinning end-over-end as it travels through space.

SUMMARIZING

B. Complete the summary with the phrases in the box. One is extra.

a. alien technology	b. a cucumber	c. another star system
d. a rock	e. its speed and direction	f. our solar system

In October 2017, astronomers saw a strange object that was shaped like [1]_____.

By studying [2]_____, the scientists realized that the object had come from [3]_____.

The object was called 'Oumuamua. Most scientists think it was just [4]_____.

However, others—such as Abraham Loeb—have suggested it could be a piece of [5]_____.

Scanning

You scan a text when you want to find specific information. When you scan, you only look for the information you want. You don't read the rest of the text. For example, for the question *What does 'Oumuamua mean in Hawaiian?*, look through the text for the words *'Oumuamua* and *Hawaiian*, and possibly quotation marks (" ").

SCANNING **A.** Look back at Reading A. Find and underline these words in the passage as quickly as you can.

1. Hawaii   2. surprising   3. theory
4. alien   5. solar system   6. likely

SCANNING **B.** Read the questions below. Think about what answers you need to look for. Then scan Reading A and the infographic on page 10, and write the answers.

1. When did astronomers first see 'Oumuamua?   _____
2. What does 'Oumuamua mean in Hawaiian?   _____
3. When did 'Oumuamua's speed increase?   _____
4. What is Abraham Loeb's job?   _____
5. Where does Abraham Loeb work?   _____
6. When did 'Oumuamua enter the inner solar system? _____
7. What was 'Oumuamua's top speed?   _____
8. How far was 'Oumuamua from Earth when it was first seen? _____

CRITICAL THINKING Applying Ideas   What extra information about 'Oumuamua would be useful to help scientists solve the mystery? Note some ideas below. Then discuss with a partner.

_____

_____

> 'Oumuamua was first spotted by astronomers at the Haleakalā Observatory in Hawaii.

VOCABULARY PRACTICE

DEFINITIONS **A.** Read the information. Match each word in **red** with its definitions.

Crop Circles

A farmer wakes up to find something very **strange**. Someone, or **maybe** some*thing*, has made unusual shapes in his field by pushing down his crops.[1] The shapes can only be seen from the sky. These are called crop circles.

Some people think that aliens make crop circles when they land their spaceships. However, it seems clear that they are made by people. The **technology** to make them is simple—just a rope and different sizes of wood to make thick or **thin** lines.

⌃ **A crop circle is made by pushing crops down, leaving empty spaces in the field.**

Some people make crop circles so others will believe in aliens. Other people make them just for fun.

---

1 **Crops** are plants grown in large amounts.

1. _____: hard to understand or explain

2. _____: perhaps; possibly

3. _____: not wide or thick

4. _____: the use of science and machines to do things

DEFINITIONS **B.** Match the two parts of each definition.

1. If you move at high **speed**, •   • a. you hit it.

2. If you **knock** something, •   • b. you go very fast.

3. If you **pass** a place, •   • c. you learn more about it.

4. When you **explore** a place, •   • d. you do not stop there.

WORD USAGE **C.** The past tense of the verb **pass** (*passed*) is sometimes confused with the preposition *past*. Complete the sentences by circling the correct words.

1. Scientists saw a large asteroid moving *past* / *passed* Earth.

2. I *passed* / *past* by the supermarket on my way home, so I bought some bread.

3. My friend just walked *passed* / *past* me and didn't stop to chat.

4. 'Oumuamua reached its top speed as it *past* / *passed* the sun.

BEFORE YOU READ

PREVIEWING **A.** Look at the picture and read the caption. Who wrote the story of Atlantis? What happened to the island?

SCANNING **B.** Quickly scan the passage on the next page. Remember that names of people and places usually start with capital letters.

Review this reading skill in Unit 1A

    1. What names of people can you find? Underline them.

    2. What names of places are mentioned? Circle them.

THE LOST CITY OF ATLANTIS

▽ Long ago, the Greek writer Plato wrote about Atlantis—an island that disappeared into the sea.

A   Most people have heard the story of the **lost** city of Atlantis. But is any part of the story true?

B   Over two thousand years ago, the Greek writer Plato wrote about Atlantis, an island in the Atlantic Ocean. The island's people were very rich. They built a big city with many great buildings. But the people became greedy—they had many things, but they still wanted more. So the gods became angry. Earthquakes[1] and large waves began to **strike** the island. **Finally**, Atlantis **sank** into the sea.

C   Many explorers have looked for Atlantis. In 2004, explorer Robert Sarmast **reported** finding the remains[2] of a city under the sea near Cyprus. However, Sarmast and other scientists later realized the structures he found under the sea were **natural**, not man-made. Mark Adams, author of the 2016 book *Meet Me in Atlantis* believes the city was in Morocco. Plato wrote about red and black stone circles around the city. Adams found similar red and black stones in the desert there, very near the Atlantic Ocean.

D   Most people, however, think Atlantis is simply a story. The **purpose** of the story may be to teach people not to be greedy. Richard Ellis also wrote a book about Atlantis in 1999. He says "there is not a **piece** of solid evidence"[3] for a real Atlantis.

E   So was the island real or not? We only know one thing: The mystery of Atlantis will be with us for a long time.

---

1   An **earthquake** is the shaking of the ground caused by movement of the Earth.

2   The **remains** of something are the parts that are left after most of it is gone.

3   **Evidence** is anything that makes you believe that something is true.

A. Choose the best answer for each question.

GIST

1. What could be another title for the reading?

   a. Atlantis Sinks

   b. Is Atlantis Real?

   c. I Found Atlantis!

SEQUENCE

2. What happened after Robert Sarmast said he found Atlantis?

   a. He wrote a book about his findings.

   b. Richard Ellis said that Atlantis was not real.

   c. He found out the structures were not man-made.

MAIN IDEA

3. What is the main idea of paragraph C?

   a. Scientists believe Atlantis is just a story.

   b. Explorers found a city under the sea near Morocco.

   c. People have looked for Atlantis, but no one has found it.

∧ The story of Atlantis was first written down in Plato's *Dialogues* in 360 B.C.

DETAIL

4. Why does Mark Adams believe Atlantis could be in Morocco?

   a. He discovered the remains of houses in the ocean there.

   b. He found colored stones similar to ones described by Plato.

   c. He found a map that showed Atlantis's location in the Atlantic Ocean.

PARAPHRASING

5. In paragraph D, which sentence is closest in meaning to *"there is not a piece of solid evidence"* for a real Atlantis?

   a. There is only one reason to believe the Atlantis story is true.

   b. The story of Atlantis is made up of many small pieces.

   c. There is nothing to make us believe the Atlantis story is true.

SCANNING

Review this reading skill in Unit 1A

B. Write short answers to the questions below. Use words from the passage for each answer.

1. When did Plato write about Atlantis? _____

2. When did Robert Sarmast report finding the remains of a city? _____

3. What was the title of Mark Adams's book? _____

4. Which author thinks Atlantis is just a story? _____

Skimming

You skim when you look quickly at the whole reading to see what it is about. You do not read every word. Instead, look at the title, headings, photos, and captions. Read the first line of each paragraph, and quickly read the conclusion.

SKIMMING OR SCANNING

A. Look at these reasons for reading. For each reason, should you skim or scan? Check (✓) the correct boxes.

	Skim	Scan
1. to see if a story is funny or serious	☐	☐
2. to find the names of countries mentioned	☐	☐
3. to find a quote (" ") by a scientist	☐	☐
4. to see how the author feels about a topic	☐	☐

SKIMMING

B. Quickly skim the passage below. What is it mainly about? Circle the correct option.

a. A diver who found Atlantis in the Pacific Ocean

b. A scientist who believes he has found a lost land near Japan

c. A strange structure that was found in a Japanese city

The Lost Continent in the Pacific Ocean

People believe that thousands of years ago the lost continent of Mu sank because of an earthquake. Today, no one knows if there really was a place called Mu, or where it was.

However, Professor Masaaki Kimura thinks he knows where the remains of Mu are. He believes they are near the Yonaguni Islands of Japan. Kimura thinks the strange structures he has found were made by people. Some other researchers don't think so. No one is sure, but the research continues.

⌃ **A diver explores the strange steplike structures in the waters near the Yonaguni Islands.**

CRITICAL THINKING Synthesizing Information   Which mystery do you think will be more difficult to solve: Atlantis or 'Oumuamua? Why? Note your ideas below. Then discuss with a partner.

_____

_____

_____

DEFINITIONS **A.** Read the information. Match each word in **red** with its definition.

Some people believe the Greek island of Santorini is the likely location for the **lost** city of Atlantis. The two are similar in several ways.

Plato described Atlantis as being in the shape of a circle. In the past, Santorini was also circular. However, the island was **struck** by earthquakes and nearly destroyed by a volcano, causing parts of the island to **sink**. There were also people living in cities on Santorini for thousands of years.

∧ **The Greek island of Santorini viewed from above**

There are, however, important differences. First of all, the dates in Plato's writing do not match with events on Santorini. Plato also said Atlantis was in the Atlantic Ocean, but Santorini is in the Mediterranean Sea. And **finally**, the sizes of the two islands are very different. Atlantis was described as very large, but Santorini is small.

1. _____: lastly, in the end

2. _____: unable to be found

3. _____: suddenly hit

4. _____: to move slowly downwards, often in water.

COMPLETION **B.** Complete the sentences. Circle the correct options.

1. Something **natural** is *made / not made* by humans.

2. A **piece** of something is *all / part* of it.

3. To find out the **purpose** of something, you should ask *"Where?" / "Why?"*

4. When you **report** something, you *don't tell / tell* others about it.

WORD FORMS **C.** Many verbs, such as **sink** and **strike**, have irregular past forms. Complete the sentences using the words in the box.

sink	sank	strike	struck

1. Last night, large waves _____ the side of the ship.

2. If you drop coins in water, they _____.

3. Earthquakes often _____ in countries along the Pacific.

4. Sadly, their small boat _____ in the storm.

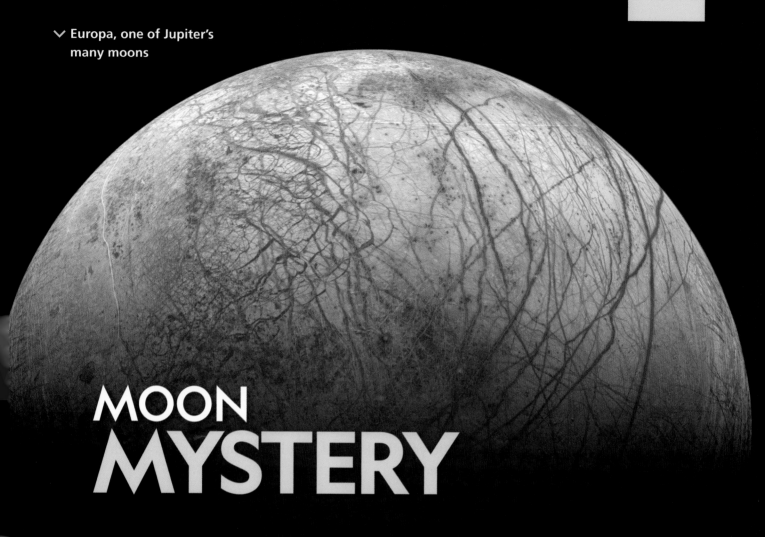

∨ **Europa, one of Jupiter's many moons**

MOON
MYSTERY

BEFORE YOU WATCH

PREVIEWING **A.** Read the information. The words in **bold** appear in the video. Complete the definitions with the correct form of each word.

For many years, scientists have searched for life in space. Spacecrafts have been sent to every planet in the solar system, and robots have landed on the **surfaces** of Mars and Venus. So far, nothing has been found. Many believe, however, that the best places to look for life might not be planets at all. Europa—one of Jupiter's many moons—is thought to have **conditions** where life may **exist**. Whether it does or not remains a mystery for now.

1. If something _____, it stays alive.

2. The _____ of something is the outside part of it.

3. The _____ of a place include things like its temperature or weather.

DISCUSSION **B.** Why do you think scientists believe there might be life on Europa? What conditions might exist there? Note your ideas. Then discuss with a partner.

_____

GIST **A.** Watch the video. Why do scientists believe Europa is a good place to look for life? Choose the correct answer.

a. ☐ It may have an ocean beneath its surface.

b. ☐ Its surface temperature is similar to Earth's.

c. ☐ It is a similar size to Earth's moon.

DETAILS **B.** Watch the video again. Complete the notes.

Discovered by Galileo in ¹_____

Slightly smaller than ²_____

Europa

Surface covered in ³_____

Future missions may send a(n) ⁵_____ to Europa.

Life has been found on ⁴_____ in similar conditions.

CRITICAL THINKING Applying Ideas   Consider what you know about the conditions on Europa. If scientists do find life there, what do you think it will look like? Note your ideas or draw a picture. Explain your ideas to a partner.

_____

_____

_____

VOCABULARY REVIEW

Do you remember the meanings of these words? Check (✓) the ones you know. Look back at the unit and review any words you're not sure of.

Reading A

☐ explore   ☐ knock   ☐ maybe   ☐ pass

☐ speed   ☐ strange   ☐ technology* ☐ thin

Reading B

☐ finally*   ☐ lost   ☐ natural   ☐ piece

☐ purpose   ☐ report   ☐ sink   ☐ strike

* Academic Word List

EATING EXTREMES

Cooks prepare a 2-kilometer-long pizza as part of a world record attempt in Naples, Italy.

WARM UP

Discuss these questions with a partner.

1. Have you ever eaten any unusual food?

2. What's the hottest (spiciest) food you've ever eaten?

The Nathan's Famous Hot Dog Eating Contest is held every year on the Fourth of July in New York, United States.

BEFORE YOU READ

PREVIEWING **A.** Look at the photo and read the caption. What kind of competition is it? Where and when does it take place?

PREDICTING **B.** How many hot dogs do you think one person can eat in 10 minutes? Discuss your ideas with a partner. Scan the passage on pages 23–24 to check your ideas.

THE WORLD OF SPEED EATING

A Competitive eating—or speed eating—is **exactly** what its name suggests. Contestants[1] eat as much as they can, usually within a time limit. Eating competitions can involve **various** foods—pizza, pies, ice cream, chili peppers. They can also offer large prizes to the winners.

The Biggest Competition

B The world's largest competitive eating event is Nathan's Famous Hot Dog Eating Contest. The event is held every Fourth of July in Brooklyn, New York. According to legend,[2] this tradition began over a hundred years ago. Four immigrants[3] were **arguing** about who loved their new country the most. Finally, they **worked out** a way to decide. They would see who could eat the most of a famous American food—the hot dog. James Mullen, an Irish immigrant, won by eating 13 hot dogs in 12 minutes. Nathan's Fourth of July **tradition** was born.

---

1 A **contestant** is someone who takes part in a competition.
2 A **legend** is a traditional story that may or may not be true.
3 An **immigrant** is someone who has left one country to live in another.

Eating Champions

C The current champion* of the contest is Joey Chestnut. Chestnut—an American—also holds the world **record** for hot dog eating—74 in less than 10 minutes. That's just over 8 seconds per hot dog. For many years, the Nathan's Contest champion was Takeru Kobayashi from Japan. He is smaller and lighter than Chestnut, and doesn't look like an eating champion. However, he holds many world records for eating different types of food.

Bad Taste or Just Sport?

D Not everybody thinks competitive eating is a good thing. It can be **unhealthy** for the contestants, and many people in the world are going hungry. Kobayashi first won the event in 2001 when he was 23 years old. So are eating competitions in bad taste? For competitive eaters, it's a sport like any other. As Kobayashi says, "Food fighters … think of themselves as **athletes**."

* as of 2018

KOBAYASHI'S WORLD RECORDS

- **15½** pizzas in **12** minutes
- **150** rice balls in **30** minutes
- **93** hamburgers in **8** minutes
- **159** tacos in **10** minutes
- **13** grilled cheese sandwiches in **1** minute

"I know I have a special stomach," says Takeru Kobayashi.

A. Choose the best answer for each question.

GIST

1. What is the reading mainly about?

  a. the history of hot dogs in the United States

  b. the career of a famous competitive eater

  c. eating competitions and the people who take part

PURPOSE

2. What is the purpose of paragraph B?

  a. to give details about a famous competitive eating event

  b. to explain how competitive eaters can eat so quickly

  c. to describe the dangers of competitive eating

DETAIL

3. What is NOT true about Joey Chestnut?

  a. He is smaller than Takeru Kobayashi.

  b. He has won Nathan's Famous Hot Dog Eating Contest.

  c. He broke the world record for hot dog eating.

PARAPHRASING

4. In paragraph D, which word could replace *in bad taste*?

  a. wrong

  b. dangerous

  c. exciting

∧ **Joey Chestnut is one of the world's most successful speed eaters.**

INFERENCE

5. Which of the following would Takeru Kobayashi most likely say?

  a. "Competitive eating is just a fun hobby for me. Winning isn't important."

  b. "I see competitive eating as a sport, and I always try my best."

  c. "Eating so much food is unhealthy. Eating competitions should be stopped."

SCANNING

Review this reading skill in Unit 1A

B. Scan the passage for the names in the box. Match each person (a–c) with the sentence that describes them. Each person may be used more than once.

a. James Mullen	b. Joey Chestnut	c. Takeru Kobayashi

1. _____ helped start the tradition of hot dog eating contests.

2. _____ won the 2018 Nathan's Famous Hot Dog Eating Contest.

3. _____ was born in Ireland.

4. _____ holds a record for eating hamburgers.

Identifying the Parts of a Passage

A reading passage can have several parts. Look at every part to get a complete understanding of the passage. This is very useful when previewing a passage or predicting what it contains.

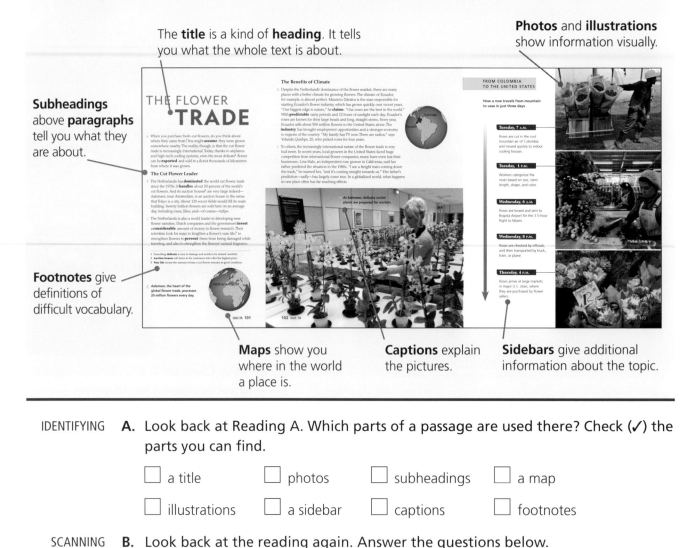

The **title** is a kind of **heading**. It tells you what the whole text is about.

Photos and **illustrations** show information visually.

Subheadings above **paragraphs** tell you what they are about.

Footnotes give definitions of difficult vocabulary.

Maps show you where in the world a place is.

Captions explain the pictures.

Sidebars give additional information about the topic.

IDENTIFYING **A.** Look back at Reading A. Which parts of a passage are used there? Check (✓) the parts you can find.

- ☐ a title
- ☐ photos
- ☐ subheadings
- ☐ a map
- ☐ illustrations
- ☐ a sidebar
- ☐ captions
- ☐ footnotes

SCANNING **B.** Look back at the reading again. Answer the questions below.

1. What is the title of the reading? _____
2. How many paragraphs are there in the main text? _____
3. Does every photo have a caption? _____
4. How many footnotes are there? _____
5. Whose records are in the sidebar? _____

CRITICAL THINKING Justifying Opinions   Discuss with a partner. The author asks if some eating contests are "in bad taste." What do you think? Would you ever enter one?

VOCABULARY PRACTICE

DEFINITIONS **A.** Complete the information. Circle the correct options.

1. An example of an **athlete** is a *singer / soccer player*.
2. People sometimes **argue** when they *agree / disagree* about something.
3. When you **work out** something, you *find the answer / tell a story*.
4. If something is **unhealthy**, it is *bad / good* for you.

COMPLETION **B.** Complete the information using the words in the box. Two words are extra.

argue	athlete	exactly	records	tradition	various

Every year, the small Czech town of Vizovice holds a festival to celebrate the plums grown in the area. The festival has a long ¹_____, recently celebrating its 50th year. One of its most popular events is a plum dumpling eating contest.

In 2017, American Patrick Bertoletti won the contest. He ate ²_____ 198 dumplings in one hour. Bertoletti has held ³_____ other world ⁴_____ in speed eating. He won the 2015 Wing Bowl when he ate an amazing 444 chicken wings in just 26 minutes.

∧ **Patrick Bertoletti shows off his Wing Bowl championship ring after winning the 2015 event.**

COLLOCATIONS **C.** The prepositions in the box can be used with the verb **argue**. Complete the sentences using the correct prepositions.

about	for	with

1. The people in the eating contest argued _____ the rules.
2. The customer argued _____ the server because his food came out cold.
3. The kitchen workers argued _____ more money because they make very little.

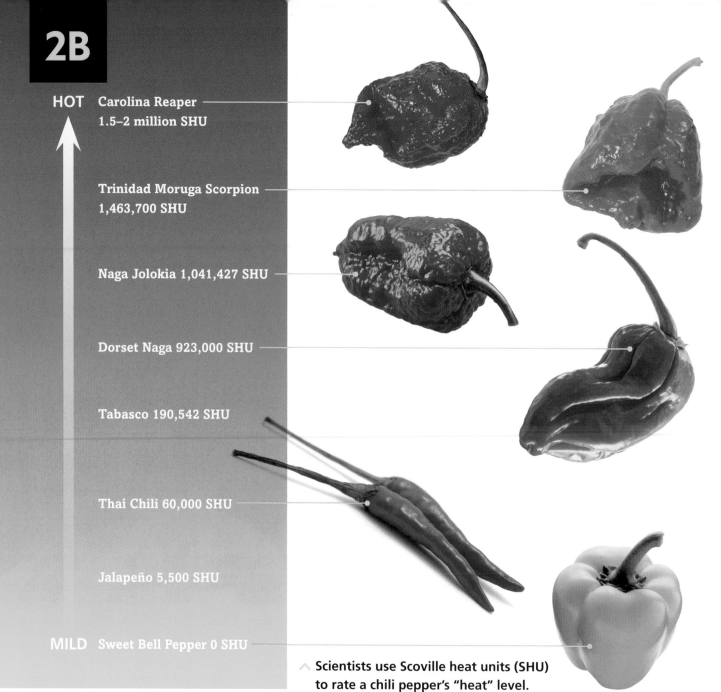

2B

HOT Carolina Reaper
1.5–2 million SHU

Trinidad Moruga Scorpion
1,463,700 SHU

Naga Jolokia 1,041,427 SHU

Dorset Naga 923,000 SHU

Tabasco 190,542 SHU

Thai Chili 60,000 SHU

Jalapeño 5,500 SHU

MILD Sweet Bell Pepper 0 SHU

^ Scientists use Scoville heat units (SHU)
to rate a chili pepper's "heat" level.

BEFORE YOU READ

TRUE OR FALSE **A.** Look at the information above. Is each sentence below true or false?
Circle **T** (true) or **F** (false).

1. The Trinidad Moruga Scorpion is hotter than the Dorset Naga. **T   F**
2. A chili pepper that measures 5,000 SHU is very hot. **T   F**
3. Tabasco peppers are hotter than jalapeños. **T   F**
4. Sweet bell peppers have a very high SHU level. **T   F**

SCANNING **B.** In Assam, India, a woman named Anandita Dutta Tamuly likes to eat very
hot chilies. Quickly scan the passage on the next page. Which of the chilies
above is she famous for eating?

Review this
reading skill
in Unit 1A

THE HOTTEST CHILIES

A You may have experienced the feeling. Your mouth feels like it's on fire. Your eyes start to water. You just ate one of nature's hottest foods—the chili pepper!

B Chili peppers, also called chilies, are found in **dishes** around the world. They are in dishes like Indian curries, Thai tom yum soup, and Mexican enchiladas. Chilies come from the capsicum **plant**. They are "hot" because they **contain** something called *capsaicin*.

C Capsaicin is very good for your **health**. It helps you **breathe** better, and it may even help keep you **fit**. Capsaicin makes you feel less **hungry**. It also makes your body burn more calories.[1]

D We can measure the heat of chilies in units called Scoville heat units (SHU). The world's hottest chili is the Carolina Reaper. It sometimes measures up to 2 million SHU!

E Eating a hot chili can be **painful**, but some people love to eat them. Anandita Dutta Tamuly, a woman from Assam, India, became famous for eating chilies. She ate 51 hot peppers in just two minutes! The peppers were Naga Jolokia ("ghost peppers"). They grow in Assam and are the third-hottest chilies in the world.

F "I found eating chilies was a great way to stay healthy," says Tamuly. She began eating chilies when she was a child. She eats chilies when she is sick, too. "Every time I have a cold or flu, I just eat some chilies and I feel better. To be honest, I barely notice them now."

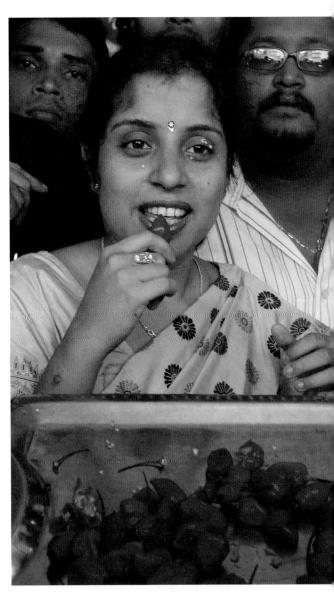

⌃ **Anandita Dutta Tamuly eats a tray full of Naga Jolokia, or "ghost peppers."**

---

1 **Calories** are units used to measure the energy value of food.

A. Choose the best answer for each question.

GIST

1. What is the reading mainly about?

a. how to eat very hot chili peppers
b. facts about hot chili peppers
c. ideas for cooking using chili peppers

PURPOSE

2. What is the purpose of paragraph C?

a. to explain why eating chilies is painful
b. to show the effect of chilies on the mind
c. to explain how chilies are good for you

DETAIL

3. How is capsaicin good for your health?

a. It helps you breathe better.
b. It makes you feel happier.
c. It makes you feel hungrier.

DETAIL

4. Which of the following is NOT true about Anandita Dutta Tamuly?

a. She is famous for eating Carolina Reaper chilies.
b. She often eats chilies when she feels sick.
c. She started eating chilies when she was a child.

PARAPHRASING

5. In paragraph F, the phrase *I barely notice them* can be replaced with _____

a. I usually don't eat hot chilies anymore.
b. I feel the heat of the chilies even more.
c. I almost don't feel the heat of the chilies.

^ **Many types of chilies turn from green to red as they grow.**

MATCHING **B. Look back at the information in Reading B. Match each pepper (a–d) with the correct description.**

a. Sweet Bell Pepper	b. Naga Jolokia	c. Tabasco	d. Carolina Reaper

1. _____ is the hottest chili in the world.

2. _____ is around 3 times the SHU of Thai Chili.

3. _____ is not as hot as jalapeño.

4. _____ is also known as "ghost pepper."

Pronoun Reference

Pronouns are words such as *he, she, it, they,* and *them,* and usually refer to a noun earlier in a passage. To understand a passage, it is important to know what each pronoun refers to.

Sara bought chilies. **She** *put* **them** *in my favorite curry.* **It** *was too hot to eat!*

REFERENCE **A.** In each sentence, draw an arrow from the pronoun in **bold** to the word it refers to, as in the examples above.

1. The jalapeño is a popular chili from Mexico. **It** takes its name from Jalapa, in Veracruz.

2. My brother and sister asked my mother not to put chilies in the food **she** made.

3. Chilies have been eaten in the Americas for thousands of years. Nowadays, **they** are popular all around the world.

4. Indians put chili peppers in many of their dishes. They often add **them** to curries.

People in the Americas were eating chilies as early as 7500 B.C.

REFERENCE **B.** Look back at Reading B. Find the following sentences in the passage. Write the word each pronoun in **bold** refers to.

1. Your mouth feels like **it**'s on fire. (paragraph A)   it = _____

2. **It** helps you breathe better. (paragraph C)   It = _____

3. She began eating chilies when **she** was a child. (paragraph F)   she = _____

4. To be honest, I barely notice **them** now. (paragraph F)   them = _____

CRITICAL THINKING Applying Ideas

▶ Work with a partner. Think of four famous spicy foods. List them below.

_____   _____   _____   _____

▶ Now rank the foods in your list from 1–4 (1 = the hottest).

COMPLETION **A.** Complete the information using the words in the box.

contains	dishes	health	painful	plants

They may not look tasty, but some types of cactus ¹_____ can be eaten and are very good for your ²_____. In Mexico, *nopalitos*—young stems of the cactus—have been eaten for hundreds of years.

Eating cactus has recently become more popular outside of Mexico. There are many tasty ³_____ that use cactus stems. Here is one way to cook them.

- Clean and cut up the stems. Don't cut yourself on the sharp parts of the plant! That can be ⁴_____.

- Next, heat some oil in a pan and add the cactus. Then add some salt and cover the pan.

- The cactus ⁵_____ a strange liquid. Cook the cactus until all the liquid comes out and dries up. Then enjoy!

∧ **A man cuts and cleans cactus stems in a Mexican market.**

DEFINITIONS **B.** Match each word in **red** with its definition.

1. **plant**   •   • a. healthy and strong
2. **hungry** •   • b. needing food
3. **breathe** •   • c. a living thing that usually grows in the ground
4. **fit**   •   • d. to take air in and out

COLLOCATIONS **C.** The words in the box are often used with the adjective **painful**. Complete the sentences using the correct words.

cut	lesson	memory

1. Looking at the old photo brought back a painful _____.
2. The chef's knife slipped, so he got a painful _____ on his hand.
3. Failing my first exam was a painful _____. I'll study harder for the next one.

SCIENCE OF TASTE

∧ A tea buyer tastes a selection of teas.

BEFORE YOU WATCH

PREVIEWING **A.** Read the information. The words in **bold** appear in the video. Match each word with the type of food it describes.

1. **sweet** •   • a. potato chips
2. **salty** •   • b. candy
3. **sour** •   • c. dark chocolate
4. **bitter** •   • d. lime

PREVIEWING **B.** Work with a partner. List three more foods for each category in activity A.

_____

_____

_____

_____

GIST **A.** Watch the video. What senses do we use when we taste food? Note your answers below.

_____

_____

DETAILS **B.** Watch the video again. Complete the sentences with the words and phrases (a–d) in the box. Each option can be used more than once.

a. more bitter	b. saltier	c. more sour	d. sweeter

1. Red food tastes _____.

2. Green food tastes _____.

3. Black food tastes _____.

4. White food tastes _____.

5. Food on a round plate tastes _____.

6. Food on a square plate tastes _____.

CRITICAL THINKING Applying Ideas   Imagine you are the owner of a restaurant. You want to serve healthier food, but you still want it to taste good. What ideas from the video might help you do this? Note your ideas below. Then discuss with a partner.

_____

_____

_____

_____

VOCABULARY REVIEW

Do you remember the meanings of these words? Check (✓) the ones you know. Look back at the unit and review any words you're not sure of.

Reading A

- ☐ argue
- ☐ athlete
- ☐ exactly
- ☐ record
- ☐ tradition*
- ☐ unhealthy
- ☐ various
- ☐ work out

Reading B

- ☐ breathe
- ☐ contain
- ☐ dish
- ☐ fit
- ☐ health
- ☐ hungry
- ☐ painful
- ☐ plant

* Academic Word List

3

COOL
JOBS

An astronomer prepares for work at the Mount Wilson Observatory, United States.

WARM UP

Discuss these questions with a partner.

1. Look at the photo and read the caption. What is the person's job?

2. Do you think this job is interesting? Why or why not?

Nora Shawki achieved her lifelong **goal** of becoming an **archeologist**, but there were **challenges** along the way.

BEFORE YOU READ

DEFINITIONS **A.** Look at the photo and read the caption. Match each word in **bold** with its definition.

1. archeologist •
2. challenge •
3. goal •

• a. something you hope to achieve
• b. a difficult situation
• c. a person who finds and studies objects from the past

SKIMMING **B.** What challenges do you think Nora Shawki might have faced in her career? Discuss your ideas with a partner. Then skim the passage to see which of your ideas are mentioned.

DIGGING
FOR THE PAST

by Nora Shawki

A When I was in third grade, I watched a video that recreated the discovery of King Tutankhamen's tomb. I remember Howard Carter[1] peering through a narrow hole in the tomb with a candle. A workman asked what he could see: "Wonderful things!" Carter said. From that moment, I knew what I wanted to do with my life.

B Today, I'm **lucky** to work as an archeologist. I study the lives of people who lived in Egypt's Nile Delta. It's exciting work. Sometimes you find something that was buried three thousand years ago. Holding a piece of **history** is an **amazing** feeling.

C So I **decided** what I wanted to be at the age of nine, and I made it happen. Seems easy, right? Not quite! The road wasn't easy. I did my studies—university, then a PhD. But along the way I was told many things: I was too young, I wasn't qualified, I should **get married** and have kids. I also needed money, so I applied for six grants.[2] The first five replies I got said *no*. Six months later, the last reply came: This time it was *yes*. Finally, I could start my own excavation.[3]

D For anyone thinking about a **career**, I would say: Never give up. If you want to do something, keep trying. If people tell you *no*, use that—it will push you. At the beginning, it **hurts**. But the next *no* hurts a little less. It makes you stronger and actually helps you.

E Second, focus on your goals. And I stress *yours*. You don't have to **follow** other people. If they say something has never been done, make it happen. You may be the first to do it! There are always challenges, but you overcome them in the end.

---

1 **Howard Carter** was a British archeologist who became famous for discovering the tomb of Tutankhamen in 1922.

2 A **grant** is money given by a government or organization for a special project.

3 An **excavation** involves removing earth to search for very old objects buried in the ground.

A. Choose the best answer for each question.

GIST **1.** What could be another title for the reading?

    a. Following a Childhood Dream
    b. A Day in the Life of an Archeologist
    c. The Nile Delta's Hidden Treasures

PURPOSE **2.** What is the purpose of paragraph A?

    a. to explain the challenges Shawki faced at school
    b. to describe what was found inside Tutankhamen's tomb
    c. to explain how Shawki became interested in archeology

SEQUENCE **3.** Which of the following happened first?

    a. Shawki applied for a grant.
    b. Shawki went to university.
    c. Shawki decided to be an archeologist.

DETAIL **4.** Which of the following is NOT given as a challenge Shawki faced?

    a. Others didn't agree with her career choice.
    b. She needed to take care of her family.
    c. It was difficult to get money for excavations.

VOCABULARY **5.** In paragraph E, what does *stress* mean?

    a. a feeling you have when your life is difficult
    b. to make it clear that something is important
    c. to introduce a new idea or opinion

MATCHING HEADINGS **B.** Match each paragraph with a suitable heading.

    1. Paragraph B •   • a. Be the First
    2. Paragraph C •   • b. Stay Positive
    3. Paragraph D •   • c. A Dream Come True
    4. Paragraph E •   • d. Overcoming Challenges

> Many discoveries have been made in Egypt's
> Nile Delta, such as the Temple of Amun in Tanis.

Dealing with New Vocabulary (1)—Using a Dictionary

When you look up a new word in a dictionary, there is often more than one definition. To find the correct definition, first identify its part of speech (e.g., noun, verb, adjective, adverb). Then look at the other words in the sentence to help you find the correct definition.

MATCHING   **A.** Identify the part of speech of the word *past* in each sentence below. Then match each sentence to the correct definition.

1. Archeologists study the **past**. •   • a. (adj) previous
2. They drove **past** the museum. •   • b. (prep) after a certain time
3. I was away this **past** weekend. •   • c. (prep) beyond a certain place
4. It's 20 minutes **past** six. •   • d. (n) the time before now

COMPLETION   **B.** Circle the part of speech for each underlined word. Then look up the word in a dictionary, and write down its definition.

1. I study the lives of people who lived in Egypt's Nile Delta. (paragraph B)
   part of speech: **noun / verb**
   definition: _____

2. I did my studies. (paragraph C)
   part of speech: **noun / verb**
   definition: _____

3. The first five replies I got said *no*. (paragraph C)
   part of speech: **noun / verb**
   definition: _____

4. Second, focus on your goals. (paragraph E)
   part of speech: **noun / verb**
   definition: _____

CRITICAL THINKING Evaluating Advice

▶ Rate each piece of career advice below 1–5 (5 = great advice, 1 = bad advice).

   a. Don't worry about money. Choose a job you love.   _____
   b. It's important to get a job at a big company.   _____
   c. Don't listen to other people. Only your opinion matters.   _____
   d. Qualifications aren't important if you have talent.   _____
   e. The best way to be successful is to start your own business. _____
   f. Dream jobs rarely happen. Aim for something more realistic. _____

▶ Compare your answers with a partner and explain your reasons.

COMPLETION **A.** Complete the information using the words in the box.

career	decide	follow	history	lucky

Do you love ¹_____? If so, there are some interesting ²_____ paths that you can ³_____. Some people work as archeologists or historians. Others might ⁴_____ to work as teachers, librarians, tour guides, or researchers.

Another interesting job is that of a "living historian." Living historians work as actors at historical sites. They wear traditional clothes and speak in the language from that time. Visitors who are ⁵_____ enough to speak to a living historian can ask them questions about life at that time.

▲ A living historian wears 18th-century clothing in Virginia, United States.

DEFINITIONS **B.** Choose the correct word or phrase to complete each sentence below.

1. If something **hurts** you badly, you may *cry / smile*.
2. If something is **amazing**, it is very *bad or boring / good or surprising*.
3. When you **get married**, you have a *husband or wife / son or daughter*.

COLLOCATIONS **C.** The adjectives below can be used with the verb **get**. Complete the sentences using the words in the diagram.

1. It's easy to get _____ in the dark.
2. We need to get _____ to leave. Class starts in 10 minutes.
3. I get _____ when I work all day without a break.
4. If I feel like I'm getting _____, I take some deep breaths and count to 10.

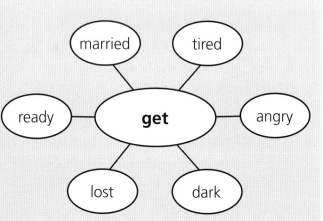

BEFORE YOU READ

DISCUSSION **A.** Look at the photo and read the caption. Then discuss these questions with a partner.

   1. What kinds of things do you usually take photos of?

   2. Do you think a photographer's job is easy?

SKIMMING **B.** Skim the interview on pages 42–43. Then write each interview question (a–d) above its answer in the passage.

Review this reading skill in Unit 1B

   a. I want to be a photographer. Do you have any advice for me?
   b. What kind of photographers is *National Geographic* looking for?
   c. Is it difficult to get a job as a photographer today?
   d. How did you become a *National Geographic* photographer?

National Geographic photographer Joel Sartore photographs an Adélie penguin chick in Antarctica.

∧ Joel Sartore prepares to take a photo
of a frill-necked lizard.

GETTING THE SHOT

An interview with Joel Sartore

A Joel Sartore is a writer, teacher, and photographer. His words—and beautiful images—show his love of photography and of the natural world. He was National Geographic's 2018 Explorer of the Year.

Question 1: _____

B My first job was for a newspaper. After a few years there, I met a *National Geographic* photographer. He liked my photos and said I should send some to the magazine. So I did. That led to a one-day job. And that led to a nine-day job, and so on.

Question 2: _____

C To get into *National Geographic*, you have to give them something they don't have. It's not **enough** just to be a great photographer. You also have to be a scientist, for example, or be able to dive under sea ice, or **spend** maybe **several** days in a tree.

Question 3: _____

D It's now more difficult to work for magazines. Technology makes it easy to take good pictures, which means there are more photos and photographers. Also, the Web is full of photos from all around the world that are **free**, or **cost** very little. These photos are often good enough to be put in books and magazines that once **paid** for photographers and their photos.

Question 4: _____

E Advice? Well, work hard. Be passionate[1] about every **project** you work on. Take lots of pictures in different **situations**. Look at others' photos thoughtfully and learn from them. And be curious[2] about life. There's something to photograph everywhere.

F But be a photographer for the right reasons. If you do it for the money, you probably won't really be happy. Do you want to make the world a better place, or make people see things in a different way? If so, you'll enjoy the work much more.

---

1 A **passionate** person has very strong feelings about something.

2 If you are **curious** about something, you want to know more about it.

A. Choose the best answer for each question.

VOCABULARY

1. In the title "Getting the Shot," what does the word *shot* mean?

 a. job   b. photo   c. magazine

DETAIL

2. Which of the following sentences about Joel Sartore is NOT true?

 a. His first job was with *National Geographic*.
 b. He once worked for a newspaper.
 c. He is also a writer.

MAIN IDEA

3. What was Sartore's main point in his answer to Question 3?

 a. Photographers need to use more technology.
 b. Putting your photos online can lead to other jobs.
 c. It's not easy to get paid work as a photographer these days.

▲ **In 2015, some of Sartore's photos were projected onto the Empire State Building, New York.**

PARAPHRASING

4. In paragraph E, the sentence *There's something to photograph everywhere* is closest in meaning to _____

 a. With new technology, anyone can be a photographer.
 b. Take more photos than you think you will need.
 c. You can find interesting things in many different places.

MAIN IDEA

5. What is the main idea of paragraph F?

 a. You should try to see people in different ways.
 b. If you work hard, you can make money as a photographer.
 c. You should ask yourself why you want to be a photographer.

PRONOUN REFERENCE

Review this reading skill in Unit 2B

B. Look back at Reading B. What does each pronoun refer to? Circle the correct option.

1. there (paragraph B)

 a. at the newspaper   b. at the magazine

2. some (paragraph B)

 a. Joel Sartore's photos   b. *National Geographic's* photos

3. them (paragraph E)

 a. different situations   b. other people's photos

4. it (paragraph F)

 a. become a photographer   b. take a photograph

Understanding Suffixes

A suffix is one or more letters that can be added to the end of a word to make a new word. The suffix usually changes the word to a different form, such as from a noun to an adjective. Knowing some of the most common suffixes can help you guess the meaning of unfamiliar words as you read. Here are some examples with their usual meanings.

Suffix	Examples
-er / -or / -ist = person who does	*painter, actor, guitarist*
-ful / -fully = full of	*colorful, playful, playfully*
-al = relating to	*musical, natural*

SCANNING **A.** Look back at the first paragraph of Reading B. Find and circle four words with the suffix *-er*.

COMPLETION **B.** In each sentence from Reading B below, underline any words that contain a suffix from the box above. Then write a simple definition of each one.

1. His words—and beautiful images—show his love of photography and the natural world.

_____

_____

2. To get into *National Geographic*, you have to give them something they don't have.

_____

3. Look at others' photos thoughtfully and learn from them.

_____

DEFINITIONS **C.** Look back at Reading A, "Digging for the Past." Find and write a word that contains each suffix below. Then write a sentence with each word.

1. -ful (paragraph A) _____   **2.** -ist (paragraph B) _____

_____

_____

_____

CRITICAL THINKING Personalizing

▶ Write three questions you would like to ask Joel Sartore.

1. _____?

2. _____?

3. _____?

▶ Compare with a partner. How do you think Sartore would answer your questions?

COMPLETION **A.** Complete the information using the words in the box.

enough	project	several	situation	spent

Stories Behind the Shots

Joel Sartore takes studio photos of animals as part of a ¹_____ called the Photo Ark. The aim is to raise awareness of endangered species. Sartore usually takes ²_____ images of the same animal, but things don't always go according to plan.

Joel Sartore took this photo of an ocelot at a zoo in the United States. He ³_____ a lot of time with the animal, but getting the shot was not easy. "They hardly ever hold still," says Sartore. "So I really had to act quickly." Many animals will stand still only long ⁴_____ to get food. After they eat, the photo shoot is over.

Behind this image is another great story. At an aquarium, Sartore came across a very angry frog. While he tried to take a photo of it, it tried to bite him. He never thought he would be in a ⁵_____ where he was afraid of a frog! "First time for everything," says Sartore.

DEFINITIONS **B.** Match the two parts of each definition.

1. When you **pay** for something,　•　　• a. it is expensive.
2. If something **costs** a lot of money,　•　　• b. you don't need to give money for it.
3. If something is **free**,　•　　• c. you give money for it.

WORD FORMS **C.** The verbs **pay**, **cost**, and **spend** have irregular past tense forms. Write the past tense form of each verb in the chart below. Then complete the sentences using the correct words.

pay → _____　　cost → _____　　spend → _____

1. I _____ in cash for my new camera.
2. It doesn't _____ much to take a photography class.
3. My parents _____ a lot of money on their new car.

> At Canine Assistants, dogs learn to be more than just pets.

RIGHT DOG FOR THE JOB

BEFORE YOU WATCH

PREVIEWING **A.** Read the information. The words in **bold** appear in the video. Match the correct form of each word with its definition.

Since 1991, Canine Assistants has **trained** over 1,500 dogs. These "super-dogs" learn more than just tricks. Once their **training** is complete, the dogs will be given to people who need help in their daily lives. These dogs have an important job to do and many things to learn. It is the animal **trainers**' job to teach them to do it.

1. _____ (v) to teach how to do a job

2. _____ (n) someone who teaches others how to do a job

3. _____ (n) the process of learning how to do a job

PREDICTING **B.** What do you think the dogs in the video learn to do? Check (✓) your ideas from the skills below.

☐ pick up things   ☐ call the police   ☐ turn lights on

☐ run in a race   ☐ open/close doors   ☐ be comfortable with people

☐ find help   ☐ drive a car   ☐ swim

☐ buy groceries   ☐ use a phone   ☐ get along with other animals

GIST **A.** Watch the video. Check your ideas in Before You Watch B.

DETAILS **B.** Watch the video again. Complete the sentences using the phrases in the box. One is extra.

a. are given food	b. are taken outside the camp	c. train in the puppy room
d. want to help their owners	e. find everything frightening	f. push a large button

1. During training, the dogs _____ when they do something right.

2. According to Jennifer Arnold, it's important that the dogs _____.

3. Before they are 16 weeks old, the dogs _____.

4. At around 8 weeks old, the dogs _____.

5. They _____ to show there is nothing to be afraid of.

CRITICAL THINKING Synthesizing Information   Look at the jobs in the box below. Consider what you've learned in this unit about each one. Which job would you most like to have? Note your ideas and explain your reasons to a partner.

archeologist	**living historian**	**wildlife photographer**	**dog trainer**

VOCABULARY REVIEW

Do you remember the meanings of these words? Check (✓) the ones you know. Look back at the unit and review any words you're not sure of.

Reading A

☐ amazing   ☐ career   ☐ decide   ☐ follow

☐ get married   ☐ history   ☐ hurt   ☐ lucky

Reading B

☐ cost   ☐ enough   ☐ free   ☐ pay

☐ project*   ☐ several   ☐ situation   ☐ spend

*Academic Word List

4

SHIPWRECKS

A diver investigates the
wreck of a sailing boat
off the coast of Egypt.

WARM UP

Discuss these questions
with a partner.

1. Do you know about any
   famous shipwrecks?

2. What do you think
   happened to the ship in
   the photo?

49

A. Look at the picture and read the timeline. Check each word in **bold** in a dictionary.

PREVIEWING **B.** Look at the picture and timeline again. Answer the questions.

1. What caused the *Titanic* to sink?

2. Why did so many people die?

3. When did explorers find the *Titanic* again? How did they study it?

SCANNING **C.** Read the first sentence of each paragraph of the reading passage on the next two pages. How many times did Robert Ballard explore the *Titanic*? Read the whole passage to check your answer.

> Called the "Ship of Dreams," the *Titanic* was the biggest passenger ship of its time.

April 10, 1912
The *Titanic* leaves England for New York.

April 14, 11:40 p.m.
The *Titanic* hits an **iceberg**.

April 15, 12:00–2:20 a.m.
Water begins to fill the ship's lower levels.
Passengers, mostly women and children, get into small **lifeboats**. But there aren't enough.

I'VE FOUND THE TITANIC!

A As a boy, Robert Ballard liked to read about shipwrecks. He read a lot about the *Titanic*. "My lifelong dream was to find this great ship," he says.

B On August 31, 1985, Ballard's dream came true. He found the wreck of the *Titanic*. The ship was in two main parts, lying four kilometers under the sea. Using video cameras and an undersea robot,[1] Ballard looked around the ship. He found many items that told the sad story of the *Titanic's* end. For example, he found a child's shoes, a reminder[2] of the many deaths that happened that night in 1912.

---

1 A **robot** is a machine controlled by a computer.
2 A **reminder** of something makes you remember it.

April 15, 2:20 a.m.
The ship breaks into two and sinks;
1,514 people die that night.

August 31, 1985 The **shipwreck** of the *Titanic* is found after 73 years. Explorers use deep-sea **submarines** to study it.

C In 1986, Ballard visited the *Titanic* again. This time, he **reached** the ship in a small submarine. A deep-sea robot took photos inside the ship. When other people saw the photos, they wanted to visit the ship, too.

D When Ballard **returned** in 2004, he found the *Titanic* in very bad **condition**. Other explorers had taken away about 6,000 items, like clothes, dishes, and shoes. Some even took pieces of the ship. They think these things should be moved to a safer place, but Ballard doesn't **agree**.

E Ballard believes that taking things from the *Titanic* is wrong. **Instead**, he wants to put lights and cameras on and around the shipwreck. This way, people can see the great ship and remember what happened to it. "As long as she needs protection,"[3] says Ballard, "the *Titanic* will always be part of my life."

▲ **Deep-sea explorer Robert Ballard**

---

3 If someone gives you **protection**, they keep you safe from danger.

< **Lights from a submarine show the inside of a first-class cabin on the wreck of the *Titanic*.**

A. Choose the best answer for each question.

GIST

1. What is the reading mainly about?

a. how visitors to the *Titanic* leave it in bad condition

b. Robert Ballard's hopes that more people will visit the *Titanic*

c. how Robert Ballard found the *Titanic* and wants to keep it safe

DETAIL

2. The first time he explored the *Titanic*, Ballard did NOT _____.

a. visit the shipwreck in a submarine

b. find a child's shoes in the shipwreck

c. use a robot to look around the shipwreck

DETAIL

3. According to the passage, what did people see that made them want to visit the *Titanic*?

a. the submarine Ballard used

b. photos from inside the ship

c. items that were taken from the ship

∧ The *Titanic* just before its first and final trip in 1912

REFERENCE

4. In paragraph D, who does *They* refer to?

a. Robert Ballard and his team

b. other visitors to the *Titanic* shipwreck

c. people from the *Titanic* who are still alive

INFERENCE

5. Which statement would Ballard probably agree with?

a. People should not remove anything from the *Titanic*.

b. Lights and cameras will hurt the remains of the *Titanic*.

c. The *Titanic* wreck should be moved out of the water completely.

SUMMARIZING

B. Complete the summary. Choose the correct options (a–f).

a. a child's shoes	b. an undersea robot	c. a small submarine
d. lights and cameras	e. thousands of items	f. very bad condition

In 1985, Robert Ballard found the wreck of the *Titanic*. He used ¹_____ to look around the ship. He found many items left by passengers such as ²_____. In 1986, Ballard visited the wreck again. This time, he reached it in ³_____. When he returned again in 2004, he found the *Titanic* in ⁴_____. Other explorers had removed ⁵_____. Ballard wants to protect the ship by putting ⁶_____ around it.

Identifying a Paragraph's Main Idea

Most paragraphs have one main idea. To determine the main idea of a paragraph, ask yourself, "What point is the author trying to make?" The first and last sentences of a paragraph, as well as its heading (if it has one), can also give you clues about the main idea.

IDENTIFYING MAIN IDEAS

A. What is the main idea of the text below? Circle the correct option.

a. The *Carpathia* took over three hours to get to the *Titanic*.
b. The *Carpathia* answered the *Titanic*'s call and helped save lives.
c. The *Carpathia* was too far away to help stop the *Titanic* from sinking.

On April 15, 1912, at 12:20 a.m., the British ship *Carpathia* got a message from the *Titanic*. The "Ship of Dreams" was sinking. The *Carpathia* was 93 kilometers away. It traveled at top speed to where the *Titanic* was, even though there were dangerous icebergs in the ocean. It arrived at 3:30 a.m., over an hour after the *Titanic* sank. Still, the *Carpathia* was able to pick up 711 people. The ship then went to New York, arriving there on April 18.

IDENTIFYING MAIN IDEAS

B. Look back at Reading A. What is the main idea of each paragraph? Circle the correct options.

Paragraph A: a. Ballard read a lot about the *Titanic*.
b. Ballard's dream was to find the *Titanic*.

Paragraph B: a. Ballard found items like a child's shoes.
b. Ballard finally found the shipwreck he was looking for.

Paragraph C: a. Ballard reached the ship in a small submarine.
b. Ballard returned and took photos of the ship.

Paragraph D: a. Some explorers had found shoes at the wreck.
b. The *Titanic* was in bad condition when Ballard returned.

Paragraph E: a. Ballard wants to protect the *Titanic*.
b. Ballard wants to put lights and cameras around the ship.

CRITICAL THINKING Evaluating Arguments

▶ The reading passage states that Robert Ballard "believes that taking things from the *Titanic* is wrong." Why do you think he feels this way?

▶ Complete the chart below with arguments for and against taking items from the *Titanic*. Share your ideas with a partner. Do you agree with Robert Ballard?

Arguments for taking items	Arguments against taking items

COMPLETION **A.** Complete the information using the words in the box. One word is extra.

conditions deaths items reach returned

Why were there so many [1]_____ on the night
the *Titanic* sank? One reason was the freezing
[2]_____. Experts believe most people who fell
into the water died from the cold in under 15 minutes.
However, the main reason was that there were not
enough lifeboats. There were 2,223 people on the ship,
but lifeboats for only 1,186 people. Also, many people
could not [3]_____ the boats before the ship
sank. In the end, only 705 people [4]_____ safely
to land.

∧ **At first, most people
could not believe the
news of the *Titanic*'s
sinking.**

COMPLETION **B.** Complete the sentences. Choose the correct words.

1. If people **agree**, they have _____ about a subject.

   a. the same idea   b. different ideas

2. If you drink tea **instead** of coffee, you drink _____.

   a. tea   b. both tea and coffee

3. An example of an **item** of clothing is _____.

   a. warmth   b. a jacket

4. A lifelong **dream** is something you have _____ all your life.

   a. wanted to do   b. tried to stop doing

WORD USAGE **C. The verb agree can be followed by the prepositions *with*, *to*, and *on*.**

You **agree with** a person (e.g., *I don't agree with you*).
You **agree to** do something (e.g., *I agreed to help my friend*).
You **agree on** something (e.g., *Everyone agreed on the cause of the problem*).

Complete the sentences. Circle the correct prepositions.

1. We couldn't agree *with / to / on* where to go for lunch.

2. I don't often agree *with / to / on* my parents.

3. Thanks for agreeing *with / to / on* work this weekend.

BEFORE YOU READ

Review this reading skill in Unit 4A

SKIMMING FOR MAIN IDEAS

A. Skim the first three paragraphs of the reading. Match each paragraph to its main idea.

1. Paragraph A •   • a. There was a problem during the expedition.
2. Paragraph B •   • b. The team came up with a plan.
3. Paragraph C •   • c. Corey Jaskolski was part of a team that explored the *Titanic*.

SKIMMING FOR MAIN IDEAS

B. Skim the rest of the reading. Was the team's plan a success? Read the passage to check your ideas.

> Corey Jaskolski and two crewmembers reached the wreck of the *Titanic* in a small submarine.

MY DESCENT
TO THE TITANIC

by Corey Jaskolski

A In 2001, I was part of an expedition[1] to explore the *Titanic*. Our team used two small deep-sea robots, one blue and one green. My job was to make sure the robots' **batteries** worked well.

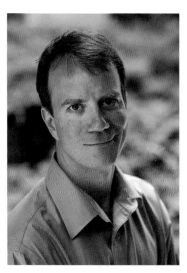

∧ **Corey Jaskolski**

B Three days into the expedition, the green robot got stuck inside the *Titanic*. Even worse, one of its batteries was damaged. That was dangerous, as the battery could explode. It could harm the robot and the ship. We had to find a way to get it out.

C In the middle of the ocean, though, there are no stores to buy supplies. So, we had an idea. We took a coat hanger[2] and put it inside the blue robot. The **plan** was to use the hanger's hook[3] to **pull** out the green robot.

D Two crew members and I got ready to go down in a three-man submarine. A crane lifted us and placed us in the water. Then we started to sink—12,500 feet to the ocean bottom. If anything went wrong, we were **totally** on our own.

E At about 9,000 feet, a crewmate accidentally touched some wires. Suddenly, all the sub's lights went out. We were in complete darkness. It was terrifying, but the **pilot** was able to **fix** it, and we **carried on**.

F Finally, we reached the *Titanic*'s wreckage. First, we could just see pieces of **metal**. Then we started to see suitcases and shoes. Over a thousand people fell here, but their bodies disappeared long ago.

G For about 12 hours, we tried to pull the robot out with the coat hanger. Finally, we got it and brought it to the surface. There was no way we were going to leave it behind. That little robot was part of our team.

---

1 An **expedition** is a trip organized for a specific purpose.
2 A **coat hanger** is an object used to hang clothes in closets.
3 A **hook** is a curved piece of metal used to attach one thing to another.

A. Choose the best answer for each question.

GIST

1. What was Jaskolski's main job?

a. to build the robots for the mission
b. to drive the robots through the wreck of the *Titanic*
c. to make sure the robots' batteries didn't stop working

MAIN IDEA

2. What was the problem with the robot?

a. It exploded and damaged the ship.
b. It was trapped inside the wreck.
c. The team lost it in the dark water.

PARAPHRASING

3. Which sentence is closest in meaning to *we were totally on our own*?

a. We had to control the robots ourselves.
b. It was a very lonely feeling in the submarine.
c. There was nobody who could help us.

DETAIL

4. What caused the problem described in paragraph E?

a. the pilot
b. a robot
c. a crewmate

VOCABULARY

5. In paragraph F, what does *fell* mean?

a. died
b. dropped
c. tripped

△ **The two deep-sea robots Jaskolski used to study the *Titanic* wreck**

SUMMARIZING

B. Complete the sentences with the options (a–c) in the box. Each option can be used more than once.

a. the blue robot	b. the green robot	c. the submarine

1. There was a problem with the batteries in _____.
2. A hook was attached to _____.
3. A crane was used to put _____ into the water
4. There was a problem with _____ when somebody touched some wires.
5. The crew eventually used _____ to pull out _____.

Recognizing Compound Subjects and Objects

A sentence can have a single subject or a compound subject. A compound subject is a subject that contains two or more nouns. Sentences can also contain compound objects. Look at the examples below.

Compound subject: (_Ballard_ and _his team_) _found the_ Titanic _in 1985._

Compound object: _Ballard used_ (_cameras_ and _a robot_) _to look at the ship._

ANALYZING **A.** Find and circle examples of compound subjects and objects in the passage below. In each example, underline the different subjects or objects.

On July 17, 1956, the _Andrea Doria_ left Italy for New York. The ship was carrying over 1,700 passengers and crew members. A week later, the _Stockholm_ left New York for Sweden. That night, the _Andrea Doria_ and _Stockholm_ crossed paths with tragic results. Just after 11:00 p.m., the _Stockholm_ smashed into the side of the _Andrea Doria_. The _Andrea Doria_ began to sink slowly. The _Stockholm_ helped with the rescue of the passengers, but there would be 52 deaths that night. Were darkness and bad weather the cause of the accident? It remains a mystery to this day.

∧ The _Andrea Doria_ sank shortly after this photo was taken.

SCANNING **B.** Find examples of compound subjects and objects in Reading B. Note them below.

1. Paragraph B: compound object: _____ and _____
2. Paragraph D: compound subject: _____ and _____
3. Paragraph F: compound object: _____ and _____

CRITICAL THINKING Evaluating Ideas   What are the advantages of sending robots to look at shipwrecks? What are the advantages of sending humans in submarines? Note some ideas in the chart below. Then discuss with a partner.

Advantages of Robots	Advantages of Humans

DEFINITIONS **A.** Read the information. Then complete the definitions using the correct form of the words in **red**.

Up to now, **battery**-powered robots have mostly explored the *Titanic*, along with a few lucky **pilots** and crew members in deep-sea submarines. For the average person, a visit to the famous wreck has only been a dream. That could change, as several companies **plan** to take visitors there in the future. The cost? Over $100,000.

Not everyone thinks these trips are a good idea, but if you decide to go, you may want to act fast. Harmful bacteria is eating away at the wreck. Some people believe that the ship could **totally** disappear in a few decades.

1. A _____ is someone who flies a plane or steers a ship.

2. A _____ is a small device that provides power for electrical items.

3. When you _____ something, you decide in detail what to do.

4. When you say _____, it means *completely* or *wholly*.

COMPLETION **B.** Complete each sentence with a word from the box.

carry on	fix	metal	pull

1. The *Titanic* was made mainly of _____. The wrecks of wooden ships do not last as long.

2. Robert Ballard says he will _____ working to protect the wreck of the *Titanic* for as long as necessary.

3. The arm of the robot sub is not working properly. Someone needs to come and _____ it before it can be used again.

4. After we finished our dive, we asked the crew to _____ us and our equipment out of the water.

WORD WEB **C.** There are many words that have the same meaning as **totally**. Complete the diagram below. Use a dictionary to help.

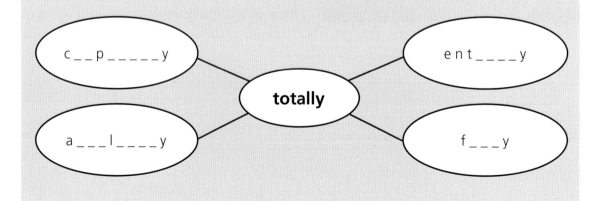

c _ _ p _ _ _ _ _ y

a _ _ _ l _ _ _ _ y

totally

e n t _ _ _ _ _ y

f _ _ _ y

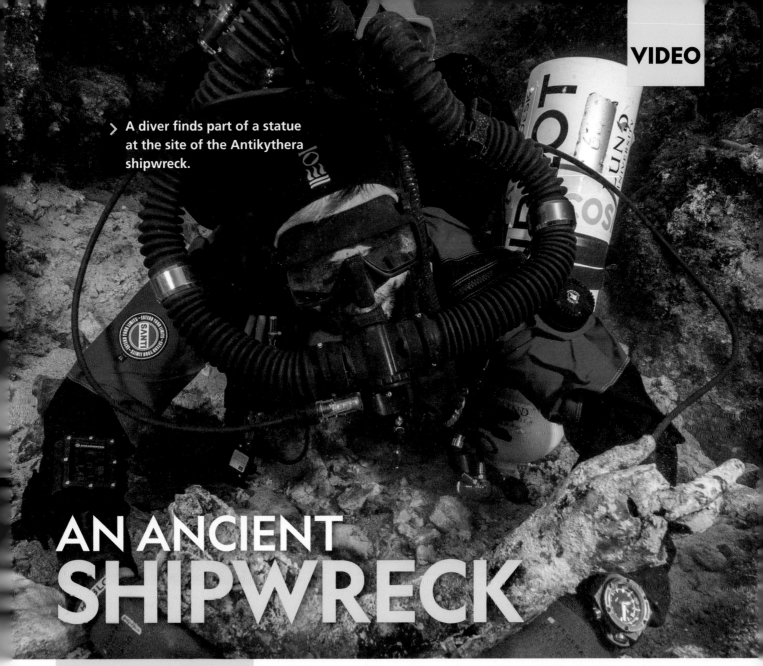

> A diver finds part of a statue at the site of the Antikythera shipwreck.

AN ANCIENT SHIPWRECK

BEFORE YOU WATCH

PREVIEWING **A.** Read the information. The words in **bold** appear in the video. Match each word with its definition.

On the **seabed** near the Greek island of Antikythera, an **ancient** shipwreck can be found. Experts believe that the ship likely sank around 2,000 years ago on its way to Rome. Since the wreck was discovered, many archeologists have visited the site. Some of the objects found include pieces of **statues** and other strange items.

1. _____ (adj) very old

2. _____ (n) models of people made from stone or metal

3. _____ (n) the bottom of the ocean

DISCUSSION **B.** What other kinds of objects do you think could be found in a 2,000-year-old shipwreck? Discuss with a partner.

GIST **A.** Watch the video. Which of the following is the best summary? Circle the correct option.

   a. A strange statue found at the Antikythera shipwreck has been a mystery for over a hundred years.

   b. Though the Antikythera shipwreck was first found over one hundred years ago, interesting discoveries continue to be made.

MATCHING **B.** Match each item in the box (a–c) with a description (1–5). Each item can be used more than once.

a. the Antikythera mechanism	b. the metal arm	c. the metal disk

1. _____ and _____ were discovered in 2017.   **4.** No one knows what _____ was used for.

2. _____ was discovered in 1900.   **5.** _____ is sometimes called an "ancient

3. _____ was used to study the stars.   computer."

CRITICAL THINKING Justifying Ideas

▶ What do you think the metal disk discovered in the Antikythera shipwreck was? Look at the possibilities in the box below. Add two of your own ideas.

a coin	a medal	a shield
a toy	_____	_____

▶ Discuss with a partner. Use information from the video to support your ideas.

∧ **An artist's drawing of the disk found at the shipwreck**

VOCABULARY REVIEW

Do you remember the meanings of these words? Check (✓) the ones you know. Look back at the unit and review any words you're not sure of.

Reading A

☐ agree ☐ condition ☐ death ☐ dream

☐ instead ☐ item* ☐ reach ☐ return

Reading B

☐ battery ☐ carry on ☐ fix ☐ metal

☐ pilot ☐ plan ☐ pull ☐ totally

*Academic Word List

SCIENCE INVESTIGATORS

WARM UP

Discuss these questions with a partner.

1. What is the investigator in the photo doing?

2. In what other ways can science help to solve crimes?

An investigator at an FBI training facility learns how lasers can be used to work out the flight path of bullets.

BEFORE YOU READ

PREVIEWING **A.** Look at the title and the photos. What do you think a "disease detective" does? Discuss your ideas with a partner.

SKIMMING **B.** Skim the reading and check your ideas in activity A.

THE DISEASE DETECTIVE

A Six children were in the hospital. They were very sick, but the doctors didn't know what to do. They called Dr. Richard Besser, an **expert** on strange **illnesses**.

Finding a Cause

B First, Dr. Besser needed to find the cause of the illness. He looked for germs[1] in the children's bodies. In every child, Dr. Besser found the same type of the bacteria *E. coli*. He then looked at the bacteria's DNA.[2] It showed him that this type of *E. coli* was **dangerous**.

C Dr. Besser knew *E. coli* could move from animals to humans. Had the children **touched** animals that carried the bacteria? Besser found other *E. coli* cases in the area where the children lived. But it wasn't enough.

D Besser then made a **list** of what the sick children had eaten. They had all eaten cheese, apple juice, and fish. He then made a list of what healthy children in the area had eaten. They had eaten the cheese and fish, but not the apple juice.

Case Closed

E Besser went to where the apple juice was made. He saw animals around the apple trees. He also saw the workers using **dirty** apples that had fallen on the **ground**. More importantly, he saw that the apples were not washed before the juice was made, and that the juice was not heated. Doing these things would **kill** the bacteria. Besser then knew it was the apple juice that made the children sick.

F Besser's *E. coli* case had a happy ending. The children got better. And what Besser learned that day now helps keep others safe.

---

1 A **germ** is a very small living thing that can cause disease.
2 **DNA** is a chemical that contains information about a living thing's characteristics.

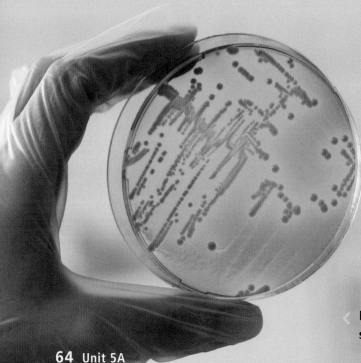

Bacteria are very small living things. Some bacteria, such as *E. coli*, can be dangerous to humans.

A. Choose the best answer for each question.

GIST

1. Another title for this passage could be _____.

    a. Good vs. Bad Bacteria

    b. Looking for Answers

    c. A Death at the Hospital

SEQUENCE

2. Which of these things happened first?

    a. Dr. Besser found out the illness was caused by *E. coli*.

    b. Dr. Besser made a list of what the sick children ate.

    c. Dr. Besser went to where the apple juice was made.

DETAIL

3. Which of the following is NOT true about *E. coli*?

    a. It contains DNA.

    b. It can make people sick.

    c. There is only one type.

CAUSE AND EFFECT

4. What made the children sick?

    a. old fish

    b. dirty apples

    c. smelly cheese

INFERENCE

5. What advice would Dr. Besser probably agree with?

    a. Never drink apple juice from a supermarket. You should make it yourself.

    b. Stay away from animals that live near trees. They will make you sick.

    c. Don't eat fruit straight from the ground. Wash the fruit before you eat it.

△ **Dr. Richard Besser is an expert on illnesses that move and kill quickly.**

SUMMARIZING

B. Complete the sentences. Use one to three words from the passage for each answer.

1. Dr. Besser knew the *E. coli* was dangerous after he looked at the bacteria's _____.

2. *E. coli* can be passed from _____.

3. The healthy children in the area had not drunk any _____.

4. There was bacteria in the juice because the apples were not _____ and the juice was not _____.

Identifying the Purpose of a Paragraph

Identifying a paragraph's purpose (or purposes) helps you understand the organization of a passage. The first line of a paragraph and its heading (if it has one) can give you clues about its purpose. These purposes can include:

- to introduce a topic
- to give an example
- to give data and statistics
- to give a conclusion
- to ask (or answer) a question
- to describe a problem
- to list a sequence of actions
- to describe a solution

IDENTIFYING PURPOSE

A. Look back at Reading A. Choose the main purpose of each paragraph.

1. Paragraph A
   a. to describe a problem
   b. to give an example

2. Paragraph D
   a. to list a sequence of actions
   b. to answer a question

3. Paragraph E
   a. to introduce a topic
   b. to answer a question

4. Paragraph F
   a. to give data and statistics
   b. to give a conclusion

IDENTIFYING PURPOSE

B. Look back at Unit 4, Reading B. Note the purpose of each paragraph below.

1. Paragraph A: _____

2. Paragraph B: _____

3. Paragraph C: _____

4. Paragraph D: _____

5. Paragraph G: _____

CRITICAL THINKING Applying Ideas

▶ Look back at paragraph E in Reading A. Write three rules that the apple juice factory should follow to make sure an *E. coli* case does not happen again.

_____
_____
_____

▶ Compare your ideas with a partner. Explain your reasons.

VOCABULARY PRACTICE

COMPLETION **A. Complete the information using the words in the box.**

dangerous	expert	illness	kill	touch

To most people, a bee sting is painful but not really

¹_____. However, for some, a little bee sting can

²_____. In fact, every year, there are many people who

die from bee stings. But scientists are learning that bee stings

can also be used to help people. Dr. Chris Kleronomos is a(n)

³_____ on natural medicines. He is trying to help a young

man named Erick. Erick has a(n) ⁴_____ that causes his muscles to hurt. He

experiences pain when people ⁵_____ him. Dr. Kleronomos uses the bee's

poison to take away Erick's pain. It may sound strange, but for people like Erick, it

seems to be working.

DEFINITIONS **B. Complete the sentences. Circle the correct words.**

1. If something is **dirty**, it is not *cheap / clean*.

2. A **list** usually has *just one thing / many things* on it.

3. If you see something on the **ground**, you are probably looking *down / up*.

4. An **expert** on a subject knows *a lot / very little* about it.

WORD FORMS **C. The suffix *-ous* can be added to some nouns to make adjectives (e.g., danger → dangerous). Complete the chart below.**

Nouns		Adjective
danger	→	**dangerous**
_____	→	adventurous
fame	→	_____
_____	→	mysterious

Now complete the sentences using the correct form of the words above.

1. My road trip through New Zealand was a real _____.

2. The doctor had no idea about the cause of the illness. It was a(n) _____.

3. If you're _____, many people will recognize you.

DEFINITIONS **A.** Look at the photo and caption. Complete the definitions using the correct form of the words in **bold**.

1. A _____ is a person who takes things they do not own.

2. A _____ is a piece of information that helps solve a crime.

3. A _____ is made when you touch something with your hands.

SCANNING **B.** Quickly scan the reading passage. Underline all the clues the crime scene investigator finds.

Crime scene investigators look for many different types of **clues,** such as objects or **fingerprints** left by a **thief.**

AT THE SCENE OF A CRIME

A It's 5:30 a.m., and your phone rings. A police officer says someone broke into[1] a store and took some expensive items. They need you right away. It is your job to study the whole scene for clues that will help **catch** the thief. You are a crime scene investigator, and the game is on.

B Outside the store, you see a broken window, but there is no glass on the street. There are shoeprints, and marks made by a **vehicle**'s tires.[2] You look at the shoeprints. They're large, so you're likely looking for a man. You photograph the shoe's pattern. This can tell you the type of shoe. You then measure the **space** between the shoeprints. You now know how long the person's **steps** were. This gives you an idea of how tall the thief was.

C As you follow the shoeprints over to the tire marks, the spaces between the steps get bigger. They lead to the passenger's side of the vehicle. Now you know the thief probably didn't work **alone**. You photograph the tire marks. They can help you find out the type of vehicle and the **direction** it went.

D The most important clues will come from a person's body. You find some fingerprints near the broken window. Using a computer, you can **compare** these prints against millions of others. You also find a hair. You keep it, because you know hair contains a person's DNA. You can compare this with other people's DNA, too. If you find a match for the fingerprint or the DNA, you will know who was in the store.

E Will you find the thief? You now have a lot of information, so it's **possible**. For a crime scene investigator, it's all in a day's work.

---

1 If someone **breaks into** a place, they go inside even though they are not allowed to be there.
2 A **tire** is the outside of a car wheel. It is usually black and made of rubber.

A. Choose the best answer for each question.

GIST

1. What is the reading mainly about?

a. how an investigator used clues to find a famous thief

b. what a crime scene investigator looks for at a crime scene

c. how thieves are using new technology to break into places

VOCABULARY

2. In paragraph B, what can the word *likely* be replaced with?

a. carefully

b. probably

c. comfortably

REFERENCE

3. In the last sentence of paragraph B, what does *This* refer to?

a. the size of the thief's shoes

b. the distance between the thief's shoeprints

c. the pattern on the bottom of the thief's shoes

∧ **A crime scene investigator takes a photo of a shoeprint.**

DETAIL

4. Which of the following is NOT mentioned as something the investigator can learn from the tire marks?

a. the direction the thief went

b. how heavy the thief's car was

c. the type of car the thief used

DETAIL

5. What are the most important clues that the investigator finds?

a. fingerprints and a hair

b. shoeprints and tire marks

c. an item of clothing

EVALUATING STATEMENTS

B. Are the following statements true or false, or is the information not given in the passage? Circle **T** (true), **F** (false), or **NG** (not given).

1. The thief took nothing from the store.	T	F	NG
2. There were shoeprints outside the store.	T	F	NG
3. The tire marks were made by an expensive vehicle.	T	F	NG
4. The investigator collected DNA from the scene.	T	F	NG
5. Someone heard the noise from the crime.	T	F	NG

Inferring Meaning

A text does not always state everything directly. Sometimes you need to infer meaning by "reading between the lines." You can infer meaning by using what you already know about the topic, clues in the text, and common sense. For example, in Reading B, we know there were tire marks at the crime scene, so it is likely that the thief traveled by car.

INFERRING
MEANING

A. Look at some facts from Reading B. What can you infer?

1. There was no broken glass on the street.

   a. The thief broke the window from the inside.
   b. The thief broke the window from the outside.

2. The shoeprints were large.

   a. The thief was a man
   b. The thief was a woman.

3. The space between shoeprints near the tire marks got farther apart.

   a. The thief was walking more slowly, and then stopping.
   b. The thief was walking faster, maybe running.

∧ **A police officer searches for fingerprints.**

INFERRING
MEANING

B How sure are you of these things? Check (✓) the things you can infer from the passage. Compare your ideas with a partner and explain your reasons.

1. ☐ The crime happened at night.
2. ☐ The investigator will check the fingerprints of people who work in the store.
3. ☐ The thief had help from another person.
4. ☐ The hair belongs to the thief.
5. ☐ The thief was wearing expensive shoes.

CRITICAL THINKING Evaluating Evidence

▶ Imagine the following items are also found at the crime scene in Reading B. How helpful will they be for solving the crime? Rate each one from 1 (very useful) to 5 (not useful).

_____ a rock by the window   _____ a mark made with a glove

_____ a drop of blood near the window   _____ a drop of oil from the car

_____ a cellphone on the road outside   _____ a flashlight on the store floor

▶ Discuss your ideas with a partner.

COMPLETION **A.** Complete the information. Circle the correct words.

We know that one of the best ways to
¹**catch** / **step** a thief is by collecting
fingerprints from a crime scene and then
²**comparing** / **stepping** them to others
with a computer. But how difficult is it to get
the prints?

Try this: Press a finger onto a drinking glass.
If your fingers are oily or wet, the print will
be better. Then cover the print and the
³**direction** / **space** around it with a small
amount of powder. You can use things you have in
your kitchen, such as flour or cocoa powder.

Now remove some of the powder with a small,
dry paintbrush until you see the print. Then
place some tape over the print. Take the tape
off and put it on a piece of paper. If ⁴**alone** /
possible, use colored paper. You should now see the fingerprint clearly.

∧ **Powder is used to cover the
pattern of the fingerprint so it
can be seen clearly.**

DEFINITIONS **B.** Complete the sentences. Circle the correct options.

1. If you are **alone**, you are with *no / one or more* other people.
2. You use your *hands / feet* to take a **step**.
3. An example of a **vehicle** is a *house / bus*.
4. The **direction** of a moving object is the *general line it follows / place it
   started from*.

WORD FORMS **C.** The box below shows the different word forms of the word **possible**.
Complete the sentences using the words in the box.

possible (adj)   **possibly** (adv)   **possibility** (n)

1. There is a strong _____ that the thief is a woman.
2. The thief _____ left the scene in a large car.
3. It's _____ that no one will ever catch the thief.

The flu virus affects millions of people around the world each year.

THE FLU VIRUS

BEFORE YOU WATCH

PREVIEWING **A.** Read the information. The words in **bold** appear in the video. Match each word with its definition.

Flu—or influenza—is a **virus** that you've probably had before. If you have the flu, you might have a fever, a headache, a cough, or a sore throat. Usually, you'll feel better after a few days, but some types of flu can be **deadly**. Flu can also **spread** very quickly and can affect a large number of people.

1. deadly   •   • a. (n) a small living thing that makes you feel ill

2. spread   •   • b. (adj) able to kill

3. virus   •   • c. (v) to reach a larger area

DISCUSSION **B.** Discuss the questions below with a partner.

1. Can you remember the last time you had the flu? How did you feel?

2. What is the difference between the flu and a cold?

GIST **A.** Watch the video. Complete the sentences by circling the correct options.

    1. Avian flu starts in *birds* / *pigs*.

    2. Swine flu starts in *birds* / *pigs*.

    3. Spanish flu started in *birds* / *pigs*.

DETAILS **B.** Watch the video again. Complete the information using the numbers in the box. One is extra.

5,000   36,000   200,000   375,000   50 million

    1. Flu kills more than _____ people each year in the United States alone.

    2. Since 2004, scientists have identified more than _____ different flu viruses.

    3. Spanish flu killed _____ people between 1918 and 1919.

    4. In 2009, a type of swine flu affected _____ people.

CRITICAL THINKING Synthesizing Information   Look at the jobs in the box and answer the questions that follow. Compare your ideas with a partner and explain your reasons.

a. a scientist creating a flu medicine   b. a disease detective   c. a crime scene investigator

▶ Who do you think has the most interesting job? _____

▶ Who do you think has the most difficult job?   _____

▶ Who do you think has the most important job? _____

VOCABULARY REVIEW

Do you remember the meanings of these words? Check (✓) the ones you know. Look back at the unit and review any words you're not sure of.

Reading A

☐ dangerous   ☐ dirty   ☐ expert*   ☐ ground

☐ illness   ☐ kill   ☐ list   ☐ touch

Reading B

☐ alone   ☐ catch   ☐ compare   ☐ direction

☐ possible   ☐ space   ☐ step   ☐ vehicle*

* Academic Word List

PLANTS AND TREES

6

A 4,000-year-old bristlecone pine tree in California, United States.

WARM UP

Discuss these questions with a partner.

1. Read the caption. What is special about this tree?

2. Why are trees important to our planet?

6A

DEFINITIONS   **A.** Look at the photo and read the caption. Complete the definitions using the correct form of the words in **bold**.

     1. If you _____ someone, you make them want to do something.

     2. If you _____ a tree, you put it in the ground so it can grow.

SCANNING   **B.** Scan the reading for numbers. What was Felix Finkbeiner's original tree-planting target? What is the target now?

> Felix Finkbeiner—aged 13 in this photo—**encourages** people around the world to **plant** more trees.

PLANTING FOR THE PLANET

A When he was nine years old, Felix Finkbeiner gave a class **presentation** on climate change. The young German spoke about deforestation[1] and its effect on the planet. At the end of his talk, he **challenged** the people of his country to help by planting one million trees. Nobody thought much would come of a nine-year-old's school project. Before he was 20, however, Finkbeiner's efforts had resulted in the planting of more than 14 billion trees around the world.

Der Steiger Award

At age 17, Finkbeiner gave this talk in Dortmund, Germany.

B Finkbeiner and his **classmates** began the project—named "Plant-for-the-Planet"—by planting the first tree outside their school. Other schools followed the example, and **news** of the one-million challenge spread. As a result, Finkbeiner was asked to speak at the European Parliament. Other **invitations** soon followed, and when he was just 13, he spoke at a United Nations conference[2] in New York. "We cannot trust that adults alone will **save** our future," he said in the **speech**. "We have to take our future in our own hands."

C Finkbeiner is now in his twenties, and Plant-for-the-Planet is an organization with around 70,000 **members**. It works to teach people about climate change and to encourage the planting of more trees. Germany's one millionth tree was planted long ago. The goal now is one trillion[3]—150 for every person on Earth.

D Finkbeiner continues to give talks on climate change to world leaders. "I don't think we can give up on this generation of adults," he says, "and wait 20 or 30 years for our generation to come to power. We don't have that time. All we can do is push [current world leaders] in the right direction."

---

1 **Deforestation** is the cutting down of the world's trees and forests.
2 A **conference** is a large meeting of people.
3 A **trillion** is 1,000,000,000,000.

A. **Choose the best answer for each question.**

GIST

1. What is the reading mainly about?

   a. the problems deforestation can cause for our planet
   b. how planting trees can help the environment
   c. how a young person has made a big difference to the environment

PURPOSE

2. What is the purpose of paragraph B?

   a. to give an example of the challenges Finkbeiner faced
   b. to explain how Finkbeiner's project grew
   c. to describe Finkbeiner's personality

DETAIL

3. What is NOT true about Plant-for-the-Planet today?

   a. It teaches people about deforestation.
   b. It has many thousands of members.
   c. Its aim is to plant one billion trees.

⌃ **A child plants a tree as part of the Plant-for-the-Planet project.**

REFERENCE

4. In paragraph C, what does the word *It* refer to?

   a. Plant-for-the-Planet
   b. Germany's one millionth tree
   c. climate change

PARAPHRASING

5. Which of the following is the best summary of Finkbeiner's quote in paragraph D?

   a. It will be easier to make changes when today's young people have more power.
   b. Young people today need to push those in power to make changes.
   c. Today's world leaders are a good example for younger generations to follow.

SCANNING

B. **Write short answers to the questions below. Use words or numbers from the reading passage for each answer.**

1. Who helped Finkbeiner plant his first tree?

   _____

2. In which city did Finkbeiner speak to the United Nations?

   _____

3. How many members does Plant-for-the-Planet have?

   _____

Creating a Timeline of Events

When you read a text that has a number of different events, it can be useful to put them on a timeline. This helps you understand the order in which the events happened. Look carefully at words that signal sequence like *then, after, soon, when, now,* and *once.* But be careful, because events may not always appear in the passage in the order that they happened.

SCANNING **A. Find and underline these events in Reading A.**

      a. Finkbeiner speaks to the United Nations.
      b. Finkbeiner challenges people in his country to plant a million trees.
      c. Other schools start to plant trees.
      d. Finkbeiner is asked to give a class presentation on climate change.
      e. Finkbeiner speaks to the European Parliament.
      f. Finkbeiner and his classmates plant a tree outside their school.

SEQUENCING **B. Label the timeline with the events in activity A.**

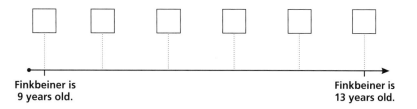

Finkbeiner is
9 years old.

Finkbeiner is
13 years old.

CRITICAL THINKING Justifying Opinions Imagine you and your classmates accepted Felix Finkbeiner's challenge to plant trees. Where is a good place to plant trees in your area? Why? Note your ideas below. Then discuss with a partner.

Children in Germany taking part in Plant-for-the-Planet

VOCABULARY PRACTICE

COMPLETION   **A.** Complete the information using the words in the box. Two words are extra.

challenge	invitations	members
news	save	speeches

Jadav Payeng lives in northeast India on the largest river island in the world. Since 1979, the river has slowly washed away much of the island. To help ¹_____ it, Payeng has planted tens of thousands of trees over the course of 30 years.

It all started when Payeng was in high school. He asked ²_____ of a local tribe if they could help with the island's problem. They advised him to plant trees and gave him 50 seeds. Forty years later, the forest stretches over more than five km².

△ **Jadav Payeng, the "Forest Man of India"**

³_____ of Payeng's success spread. Now known as the "Forest Man of India," he works to educate others and has given many ⁴_____ across the country.

DEFINITIONS   **B.** Complete the sentences. Circle the correct words.

1. Your **classmates** are people you go to *school / work* with.

2. When you give a **presentation**, you *speak / write* to a group of people.

3. If you **challenge** someone, you invite them to do a(n) *difficult / easy* task.

4. If someone gives you an **invitation**, they want you to *join / organize* an event.

WORD FORMS   **C.** Some verbs can be made into nouns by adding *-ation* (e.g., **invite** → **invitation**). Write the noun form of these verbs. Check your spelling in a dictionary.

invite → *invitation*   present → _____

transport → _____   educate → _____

prepare → _____   inform → _____

A. Look at the photo and read the caption. What does *carnivorous* mean? Check your ideas in a dictionary.

B. Do you know how Venus flytraps catch their food? Discuss with a partner. Skim the reading to check your ideas.

˅ **Venus flytraps are a species of carnivorous plant. They get most of their energy from catching and eating small insects.**

FATAL ATTRACTION

A A hungry fly speeds through a **forest**. It smells nectar[1] and lands on a green **leaf**. It starts to drink the sweet liquid. Suddenly, the fly's world turns green. The two sides of the leaf close against each other. Long green teeth **lock** together around it. The fly has been caught by a Venus flytrap. There is no escape.

B The Venus flytrap is perhaps the most **famous** killer plant. However, scientists have only recently started to understand how it hunts and eats. After years of study, plant scientist Alexander Volkov believes he now knows the Venus flytrap's secret. "This," says Volkov, "is an **electrical** plant."

C There are three small hairs **along** each of the Venus flytrap's two leaves. When an insect touches a hair, it creates an electrical signal in the leaf. The insect can continue feeding—for now. But if it touches another hair **within** 20 seconds, the trap snaps shut. This system allows the plant to tell the **difference** between a drop of water, for example, and a moving creature.

D Once trapped, an insect has little chance of survival. Instead of nectar, the Venus flytrap now releases a different liquid—one that slowly eats away at the insect. Ten days later, almost nothing is left. The plant's leaves open again, and the Venus flytrap is ready for its next meal.

---

1 Many plants produce **nectar**, a liquid that insects feed on.

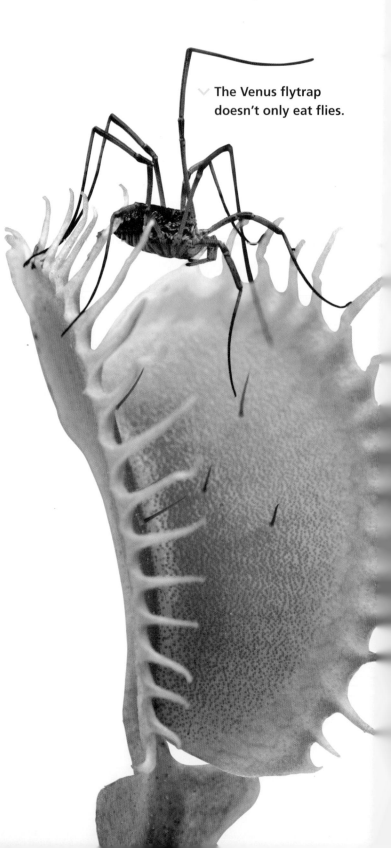

The Venus flytrap doesn't only eat flies.

KILLER PLANTS

There are around 700 species of killer plants around the world.
Here are some of the most deadly.

∧ Sundews catch insects using a sticky
liquid on the end of long hairs.

∧ A butterwort's leaves are covered with
tiny, gluey hairs that trap small insects.

∨ Pitcher plants have
long, tubelike
leaves into which
insects fall and die.

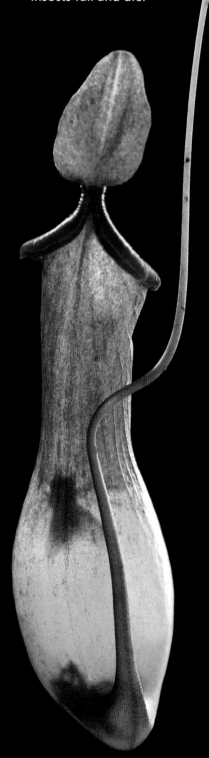

A. Choose the best answer for each question.

GIST

1. What is the reading mainly about?

   a. plants that catch and eat insects

   b. plants that are dangerous to humans

   c. how plants create nectar for insects

DETAIL

2. What is NOT true about the Venus flytrap?

   a. It can make two different kinds of liquid.

   b. It uses electrical signals.

   c. Its trap closes very slowly.

PURPOSE

3. What is the purpose of paragraph C?

   a. to explain how the Venus flytrap works

   b. to describe different types of carnivorous plants

   c. to describe an experiment carried out on a plant

INFERENCE

4. Around how many flies could a Venus flytrap eat in one month?

   a. 3 or 4

   b. between 20 and 30

   c. more than 100

△ Some pitcher plants are large enough to catch and eat small animals like frogs and mice.

DETAIL

5. Which plant does not use hairs to catch insects?

   a. the sundew

   b. the butterwort

   c. the pitcher plant

INFERENCE

B. Which of the following would cause the Venus flytrap to close? Check (✓) all that apply.

   a. ☐ A single drop of water touches a hair on a leaf.

   b. ☐ A fly touches a hair on a leaf. One minute later, it touches another hair.

   c. ☐ A fly touches a hair on a leaf. A few seconds later, a drop of water falls and touches a different hair.

   d. ☐ A small fly lands on a leaf. It drinks nectar without touching any hairs.

   e. ☐ Two small flies land on a leaf. One touches a hair. Immediately after, the other fly touches a different hair.

Understanding a Process

A process is a series of events or steps. To fully understand a process, it's important to identify the sequence of the individual events. A useful way to show the events and their relationship is to list them in a diagram.

ANALYZING **A.** Look back at Reading B. Underline any signal words or phrases that indicate a sequence (see Reading Skill 6A).

UNDERSTANDING A PROCESS **B.** How does a Venus flytrap catch its prey? Put the events in order (a–g) in the diagram.

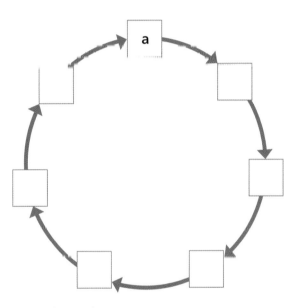

a. The plant releases nectar.
b. The trap reopens.
c. A fly lands on the plant's leaf.
d. The trap closes.
e. The plant releases a liquid to break down the fly.
f. The fly touches a second hair.
g. The fly touches a hair.

CRITICAL THINKING Applying Ideas

▶ In what ways is a Venus flytrap similar to an animal? Note some ideas below.

_____

_____

▶ Compare your ideas with a partner.

VOCABULARY PRACTICE

DEFINITIONS **A.** Read the information. Match the correct form of each word in **red** with its definition.

Like the Venus flytrap, the sundew is a killer plant. Sundews can be found in swamps and **forests** around the world. There are many types of sundews, ranging in size from a small coin to a large bush.

The sundew produces a sticky liquid that covers the hairs on its **leaves**. When an insect lands on the plant in search

⌃ **The sticky hairs on the leaf of a sundew plant**

of food, it gets stuck. As the insect tries to get free, more hairs stick to it. Some types of sundew are even able to curl their leaves over the insect and **lock** the unlucky creature **within**.

1. _____: inside

2. _____: a large group of trees

3. _____: to hold together tightly

4. _____: the flat (often green) part of a plant

WORDS IN CONTEXT **B.** Complete the sentences. Circle the correct options.

1. If there is a **difference** between two things, they are *not the same* / *the same*.

2. A *bed* / *television* is an example of an **electrical** item.

3. If something is **famous**, *few* / *many* people know about it.

4. You can walk **along** a *city* / *road*.

COLLOCATIONS **C.** The verbs *make* and *tell* are often used with the noun **difference**. Complete the sentences by circling the correct words.

1. Small changes to your diet can *make* / *tell* a big difference to your health.

2. Most people can't *make* / *tell* the difference between my twin daughters.

3. I've been waiting for three hours. Another 10 minutes won't *make* / *tell* any difference.

Giant sequoia trees in
Yosemite National Park,
United States

GIANTS OF THE
FOREST

BEFORE YOU WATCH

PREVIEWING **A.** The words in the box appear in the video. Complete the sentences using the words. Use a dictionary to help.

bark	branches	roots	trunk

1. A tree's _____ is its thickest part. It gives the tree its shape and strength.
2. The _____ of a tree grow below the ground. They stop the tree from falling down and also take food and water from the earth.
3. Most trees are covered in _____. This protects it from animals and the environment.
4. The _____ of a tree are the parts that grow outwards. They are often covered in leaves.

PREVIEWING **B.** Find examples of each word in activity A in the photo above.

GIST   **A.** Watch the video. Why do giant sequoia trees grow so big? Note three reasons below.

1. _____   2. _____   3. _____

DETAILS   **B.** Watch the video again. Complete the notes about General Sherman using numbers from the video.

General Sherman

- over ^{1}_____ years old

- over ^{2}_____ meters tall

- first branches start growing at ^{3}_____ meters

- distance around trunk over ^{4}_____ meters

CRITICAL THINKING Applying Ideas   The video says that giant sequoias "are one of the largest living things on Earth." What do you think are the other largest living things? Note some ideas below. Then discuss with a partner.

_____

_____

VOCABULARY REVIEW

Do you remember the meanings of these words? Check (✓) the ones you know. Look back at the unit and review any words you're not sure of.

Reading A

☐ challenge*   ☐ classmate   ☐ invitation   ☐ member

☐ news   ☐ presentation   ☐ save   ☐ speech

Reading B

☐ along   ☐ difference   ☐ electrical   ☐ famous

☐ forest   ☐ leaf   ☐ lock   ☐ within

* Academic Word List

7

MIND'S EYE

#aerialamerica

A 3-D drawing on the street plays tricks on our eyes and minds.

WARM UP

Discuss these questions with a partner.

1. What is unusual about the picture above?

2. Do you usually remember your dreams? What dream can you remember?

89

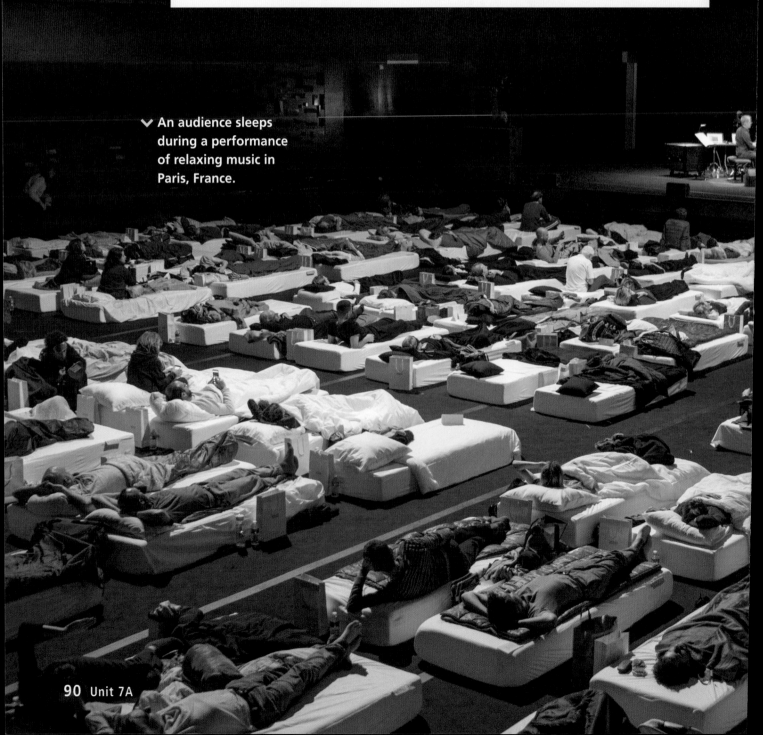

PREDICTING **A.** Many people have different ideas about what dreams might mean. What do you think it might mean if you dream about these things? Discuss your ideas with a partner.

1. You meet someone while in your pajamas.
2. You're flying.
3. You didn't study for a test.

SKIMMING **B.** Skim the reading and check your ideas.

❯ An audience sleeps during a performance of relaxing music in Paris, France.

UNDERSTANDING
DREAMS

Did you have any interesting dreams last night?

A Our dreams come from a part of the brain that contains our thoughts and **memories**. A person can have up to six dreams a night. Each one usually **lasts** from 10 to 40 minutes. Everyone dreams, but not everyone remembers their dreams. Most people dream in color, usually with sound. And we usually dream about ourselves and the people we know.

Why Do We Dream?

B Alan Siegel is a scientist who studies dreams. "[Dreams] can tell us a lot about ourselves," he says, "and can help us figure out **problems**." Another scientist, Robert Stickgold, thinks dreams come from our memories. Stickgold says that dreaming about past events is **useful** because it helps us learn from them.

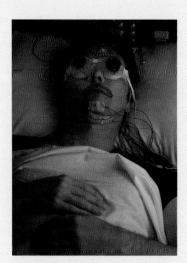

A volunteer at a dream research center

Here are a few types of dreams and what people think they mean.

Dream 1: You Meet Someone While in Your Pajamas

C This dream may be the **result** of an embarrassing[1] event in your life. Some people think we dream about embarrassing situations if our brains are trying to deal with[2] an event in our own lives.

Dream 2: You're Flying

D If you dream about flying, you are probably quite happy. This is a good **period** in your life. You may feel that other people see you as a leader.

Dream 3: You Didn't Study for a Test

E This probably means you are **worried** about an important future event. If you haven't **prepared** for it, your dream may be telling you, "It's time to get to work!"

---

1 If something is **embarrassing**, it makes you feel bad about yourself.
2 If you **deal with** a problem, you try to do something about it.

A. Choose the best answer for each question.

MAIN IDEA

1. What is the main idea of the reading?

    a. Dreams mainly come from one part of the brain.

    b. Everyone has dreams, but not everyone remembers them.

    c. We can learn a lot from the types of dreams we have.

DETAIL

2. Which of these sentences about dreams is NOT true?

    a. Dreams usually include sounds.

    b. Dreams are usually between 10 and 40 minutes long.

    c. Most people's dreams are in black and white.

VOCABULARY

3. In paragraph B, what does *figure out* mean?

    a. understand

    b. remember

    c. experience

DETAIL

4. Robert Stickgold believes that dreams _____.

    a. can tell us about our future

    b. happen more often when we're unhappy

    c. are made from our memories

INFERENCE

5. According to the passage, which of these sentences is true?

    a. If you dream you're wearing pajamas, something embarrassing probably happened to you.

    b. If you dream you're flying, this is probably a difficult time in your life.

    c. If you dream you didn't study for a test, you're probably not getting enough sleep at night.

⌃ **Most people forget half of their dreams within five minutes of waking up.**

APPLYING IDEAS

B. Read the statements (1–4). Which dream from the reading might each person have? Match each statement to a dream (a–c).

> a. You dream that you meet someone while in your pajamas.
> b. You dream of flying.
> c. You dream that you didn't study for a test.

1. _____ "Everyone at work says that I'm doing a great job."

2. _____ "The concert is tomorrow, and I haven't had time to practice!"

3. _____ "I scored three goals for my soccer team last weekend."

4. _____ "They laughed at me because I had my shirt on backwards."

Organizing Information (1)—Creating a Concept Map

A concept map helps you organize information in a visual way. To create a concept map, write the general topic or main idea of the text in the center. Then write other key ideas around the main idea. Link the ideas with lines to show how they connect. After that, add and link additional details. Generally, ideas in the middle of a concept map are more general. Ideas further from the middle are usually smaller details.

ANALYZING   **A.** Look back at Reading A. What information is important to remember? Circle the main ideas and underline the key details.

ORGANIZING
INFORMATION   **B.** Complete the concept map with information from the reading passage.

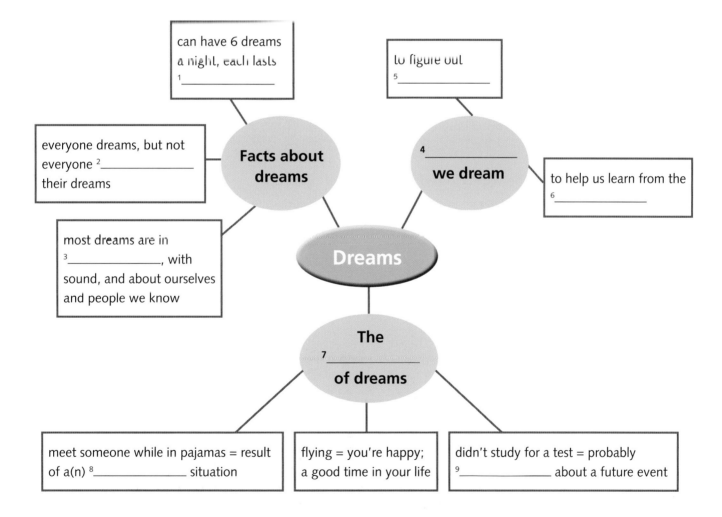

can have 6 dreams a night, each lasts
1_____

to figure out
5_____

Facts about dreams

everyone dreams, but not everyone 2_____ their dreams

4_____ **we dream**

to help us learn from the 6_____

most dreams are in
3_____, with sound, and about ourselves and people we know

Dreams

The 7_____ **of dreams**

meet someone while in pajamas = result of a(n) 8_____ situation

flying = you're happy; a good time in your life

didn't study for a test = probably 9_____ about a future event

ORGANIZING
INFORMATION   **C.** Choose a reading passage from a previous unit. Create a concept map to summarize the main ideas and key details.

COMPLETION   **A.** Complete the information using the words in the box.

lasts	periods	prepare	results	useful	worried

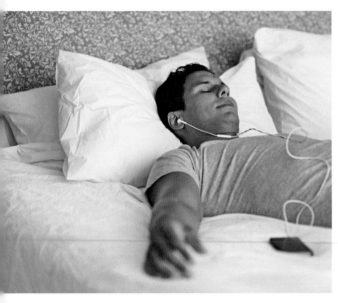

We spend about one-third of our lives sleeping. Children usually need a lot of sleep because they are still growing. Older people need to sleep for shorter ¹_____ of time. Sleep that ²_____ seven or eight hours is enough for most people.

However, a lot of people don't get enough sleep. One of the ³_____ of this is that we can become angry or ⁴_____ more easily.

If you have trouble sleeping, you can ⁵_____ for sleep by taking a warm bath or listening to slow music. Some people also find it ⁶_____ to drink warm milk.

∧ **Listening to relaxing music is a good way of getting to sleep.**

DEFINITIONS   **B.** Match the words in **red** with their definitions.

1. **problems** •   • a. a length of time in which something happens

2. **memory** •   • b. to get ready for something

3. **prepare** •   • c. things that are difficult to deal with

4. **period** •   • d. something you remember

WORD FORMS   **C.** Some adjectives that end with **-ed** can also end with **-ing** (e.g., **worried** → **worrying**). The different endings give a slightly different meaning.

I was worried. (Adjectives ending in -ed describe how you feel about a situation.)

It was worrying. (Adjectives ending in -ing describe what causes the feeling.)

Complete the sentences. Circle the correct words.
1. I find that singing in front of others is really *embarrassed / embarrassing*.
2. I read some really *worried / worrying* news yesterday.
3. Whenever I'm *embarrassed / embarrassing*, my face turns red.
4. I'm feeling really *worried / worrying* about the exam tomorrow.

BEFORE YOU READ

DISCUSSION **A.** Look at the photo and read the caption. Discuss the questions below with a partner.

    1. Can you explain what you see? How do you think this photo was taken?

    2. Have you seen photos with illusions like this before?

PREDICTING **B.** Look at the title and the pictures on the following pages. What is unusual about each picture? Discuss each picture with a partner. Then read the passage to check your ideas.

∨ This photo was taken in the middle of Salar de Uyuni—the world's largest salt flat—in Bolivia. In the dry season, the area is completely flat and white, making photos like this one possible.

SEEING THE IMPOSSIBLE

A Can you **believe** everything you see? Not always! Sometimes our **minds** and our eyes make **mistakes** and get confused.[1] This may be because we are looking at an *optical illusion.*

B The word *optical* means "related to sight"—the way we see things. An *illusion* is something that looks different from the way it really is. In short, an optical illusion is a **trick** that our eyes play on us.

C Look at these optical illusions and compare what you see with what your classmates see. The way we see things is often **personal**, so not everyone will see things the same way.

---

1 If you are **confused**, you don't understand something correctly.

1. Are the lines straight?

D At a first look, most people say "No." But if you compare the lines against an object with a **straight** edge, you'll see otherwise. The small circles in the squares help create the illusion.

2. What color are the squares?

E Square 1 is clearly gray. But what about square 2? Is it white? Is it light gray? You may not believe it, but squares 1 and 2 are exactly the same color. Your eyes see the colors, but your brain notices the shadow made by the apple. It **therefore** decides that the square in the shadow is a lighter color than it really is.

3. Are the circles moving?

F If you look closely at this picture, the circles may appear to move. Of course, this is **impossible**. How can a picture move? When we see circle-in-circle shapes, like in car wheels, they are usually moving. Our brains are used to seeing these shapes move. When our eyes see this shape, our mind decides that the image is moving. Other scientists believe the illusion of movement is caused by the movements of our eyes as we look at the different colors and patterns of the picture.

A. Choose the best answer for each question.

PURPOSE

1. What is the main purpose of the reading?

   a. to describe how human eyes work

   b. to give examples of everyday optical illusions

   c. to explain what optical illusions are and give some examples

DETAIL

2. What causes optical illusion 1?

   a. the size of the squares

   b. the color of the lines

   c. the circles inside the squares

DETAIL

3. What causes optical illusion 2?

   a. the shadow in the image

   b. the color of the apple

   c. the number of squares in the picture

∧ **By drawing a line between the two squares, you can see they are the same color.**

DETAIL

4. What is NOT given as a reason the third optical illusion appears to move?

   a. the different patterns and colors

   b. the red "Y" shapes

   c. the circular shapes

INFERENCE

5. Which of these is an optical illusion?

   a. hearing a voice in your head that isn't there

   b. seeing water on a road when it's not really there

   c. looking up at a strange cloud and noticing its shape

SUMMARIZING **B.** Complete the summary of the passage using the words and phrases in the box.

a. moving	b. our eyes and our brains	c. lines
d. they really are	e. colors	f. the same thing

Optical illusions happen when ¹_____ get confused. This means that sometimes we see things differently than ²_____. For example, optical illusions can make straight ³_____ seem to change direction. They can change the way we see different ⁴_____. They can also make an image on a piece of paper look like it is ⁵_____. However, the way we see things is personal, so not everyone experiences ⁶_____.

Understanding Conjunctions

Conjunctions are words that join ideas together in a single sentence. Recognizing conjunctions is an important part of understanding longer sentences. Here are some common conjunctions and their functions.

*I want a computer, **and** I need a printer.* (to give more information)

*I think it's gray, **but** my friend thinks it's white.* (to show how things are different)

*I might go out, **or** I might stay home.* (to show two options)

*I didn't hear her, **so** I asked her to repeat the question.* (to show a result)

*I raised my hand **because** I needed some help.* (to give a reason)

*I turned on the TV **when** I got home.* (to give a time)

*You can see a face **if** you look closely.* (to give a condition)

USING
CONJUNCTIONS

A. Complete the sentences. Circle the correct options.

1. Some people make their own optical illusions, *and / but* it's not easy to do.

2. You can find examples of optical illusions in books, *or / but* you can search online.

3. Optical illusions play tricks on the mind, *but / so* they can make people very confused.

USING
CONJUNCTIONS

B. Complete the sentences using the conjunctions in the box. More than one answer may be possible. Look back at Reading B to check your ideas.

and	because	but	if	or	so	when

1. Sometimes our minds _____ our eyes make mistakes.

2. The way we see things is often personal, _____ not everyone will see things the same way.

3. You may not believe it, _____ squares 1 and 2 are exactly the same color.

4. Your eyes see the colors, _____ your brain notices the shadow made by the apple.

5. _____ you look closely at this picture, the circles may appear to move.

6. _____ our eyes see this shape, our mind decides that the image is moving.

CRITICAL THINKING Reflecting

▶ Rank the three optical illusions in Reading B from 1 (most surprising) to 3 (least surprising).

_____ optical illusion 1   _____ optical illusion 2   _____ optical illusion 3

▶ Compare your ideas in a group. The reading passage stated that "The way we see things is often personal, so not everyone will see things the same way." Do you agree?

COMPLETION **A. Complete the information. Circle the correct words.**

Look at the photo. What do you see? Do you
¹**believe / trick** your eyes? Maybe you shouldn't.
Your eyes—and your ²**straight / mind**—might
be making a(n) ³**impossible / mistake**.

If you see only dark camels crossing the desert,
your eyes are playing ⁴**tricks / mistakes** on
you. The photographer took this photo toward
the end of the day. The sun was low in the
sky, and the camels ⁵**impossible / therefore**
had long shadows. The dark camel shapes
you see in the photo are really just the camels'
shadows. The real camels are the thin brown
shapes below the darker camel shapes.

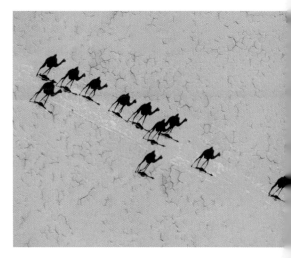

∧ **Sometimes optical illusions
happen naturally.**

DEFINITIONS **B. Complete the sentences. Choose the correct options.**

1. If an experience is **personal**, it is _____ for every person.
   a. the same   b. different

2. If something is **impossible**, it can _____.
   a. never happen.   b. happen soon

3. If a line is **straight**, it _____.
   a. creates a circle   b. continues in one direction

4. If you make a **mistake**, you do something that is _____.
   a. correct   b. wrong

COLLOCATIONS **C. The words and phrases in the box are often used with the word mistake.
Complete the sentences using the correct form of the words.**

common (adj)   **learn from** (v)   **make** (v)   **stupid** (adj)

1. It's important to _____ your mistakes in life.
2. Don't worry about it. It's a _____ mistake.
3. I think I _____ a mistake by asking my boss for a pay raise.
4. I was so embarrassed. It was such a _____ mistake!

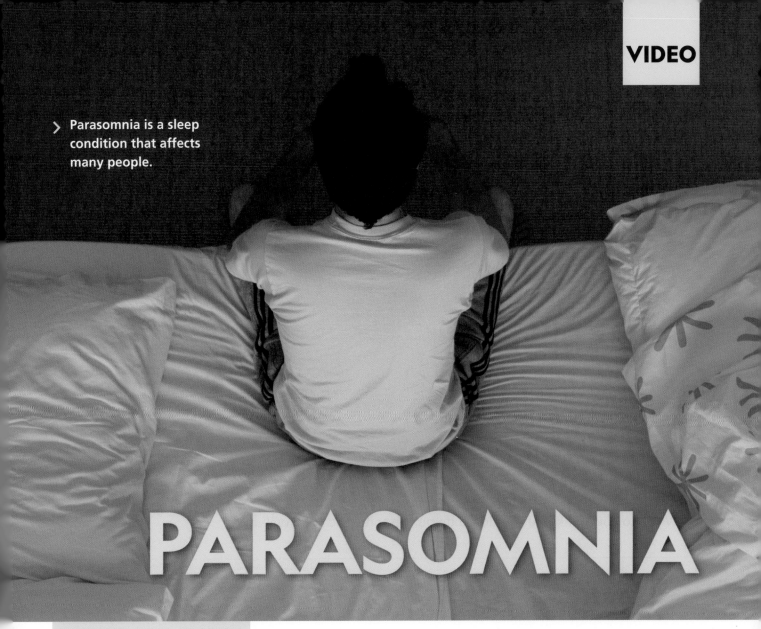

Parasomnia is a sleep condition that affects many people.

PARASOMNIA

BEFORE YOU WATCH

PREVIEWING   **A.** Read the information. The words in **bold** appear in the video. Match each word with its definition.

Sleepwalking is an example of a type of sleep **condition** called *parasomnia*. People with parasomnia may also move around in their sleep and seem to be having **nightmares**, or move their legs as if they are kicking something. Scientists know that parasomnia happens at a time in the sleep **cycle** just before people start dreaming. However, they cannot fully explain the condition.

1. condition •   • a. a bad dream

2. cycle •   • b. an illness or health problem

3. nightmare •   • c. a series of events that happens again and again

DISCUSSION   **B.** Have you, or has anyone you know, experienced any signs of parasomnia? Discuss with a partner.

GIST **A.** Watch the video. Check (✓) the sleep activities that are mentioned as examples of *parasomnia*.

☐ a. fighting ☐ b. driving ☐ c. walking

☐ d. talking ☐ e. dancing ☐ f. eating

DETAILS **B.** Watch the video again. Match the descriptions (a–e) with the stages of NREM sleep.

a. Your body relaxes.
b. Brain waves are small.
c. Heartbeat and breathing get slower.
d. Brain waves are large and far apart.
e. Your brain shuts off sounds and movements from the outside world.

Stage 1	Stage 2	Stages 3 and 4
You sleep lightly.		You're in a deep sleep.

CRITICAL THINKING Applying Ideas Note answers to the questions below. Discuss your ideas with a partner.

▶ What do you think you should do if you see someone sleepwalking?

_____

▶ What other types of parasomnia do you think can be dangerous?

_____

_____

VOCABULARY REVIEW

Do you remember the meanings of these words? Check (✓) the ones you know. Look back at the unit and review any words you're not sure of.

Reading A

☐ last ☐ memory ☐ period ☐ prepare

☐ problem ☐ result ☐ useful ☐ worried

Reading B

☐ believe ☐ impossible ☐ mind ☐ mistake

☐ personal ☐ straight ☐ therefore ☐ trick

* Academic Word List

ANIMAL WONDERS

8

A pair of meerkats look out for danger.

WARM UP

Discuss these questions with a partner.

1. What's your favorite animal? Why?

2. Do you think animals have similar feelings to humans?

BEFORE YOU READ

QUIZ **A.** What do you know about emperor penguins? Read the statements below. Circle **T** (true) or **F** (false).

1.	Emperor penguins are the biggest type of penguin.	**T**	**F**
2.	Male emperor penguins help take care of their young.	**T**	**F**
3.	Baby emperor penguins can swim as soon as they are born.	**T**	**F**

SCANNING **B.** Scan the reading. Check your answers in activity A.

⌄ **In Antarctica, home of the emperor penguin, it can get as cold as –60˚C.**

ᴬ PENGUIN'S
YEAR

A Emperor penguins are the largest penguins on Earth. Each **adult** is over a meter tall, and can **weigh** up to 40 kilograms.

B For many months each year, emperors live near the sea in large groups. However, the weather gets colder in May, and ice covers large areas of ocean. Each group moves many kilometers from the water. There, each mother penguin lays just a single egg. Then all the hungry mothers walk back to the ocean to find food. The father penguins put their eggs on top of their feet. They cover the eggs with a special piece of **skin** called the *brood pouch*.

Sharing the Work

C For two months, the father penguins protect the eggs and keep them warm. They do this through some of the coldest weather conditions on Earth. By July, it is winter in Antarctica. Most other animals leave for warmer places, but the father penguins stay.

New Life

D   By August, each mother penguin returns just in time to see her baby hatch.[1] The chick[2] is then moved to her brood pouch. This can be difficult. If the chick falls, it can **freeze** quickly. The penguin **parents** must be very **careful**. Once the chick has been moved, the father penguin can go back to the ocean to find food.

Growing Up

E   Over the next few months, penguin parents take turns[3] going to the ocean for food. They each make the trip several times, bringing back food for the chick. The chick is always hungry and grows rapidly.

Into the Water

F   By December, winter is ending. The chick can now live **on its own**. Soon it **enters** the water for the first time. It will swim and eat until next April, and then return. After a few more years, it, too, will start its own family.

---

1   If a baby animal **hatches**, it comes out of an egg.
2   A **chick** is a baby bird.
3   If two people **take turns** doing something, they do it one after the other.

A family of emperor penguins—mother, father, and baby—stands close together to keep warm.

A. Choose the best answer for each question.

GIST

1. Another good title for this passage would be _____.

a. Penguins: Sharing the Parenting
b. Penguins: Birds with Big Families
c. Penguin Babies: Swimming from Day One

DETAIL

2. Where do mother penguins lay their eggs?

a. near the sea
b. in the sea
c. far from the sea

INFERENCE

3. What is the purpose of the penguins' brood pouches?

a. to keep the eggs and baby penguins warm
b. to bring food back from the sea
c. to carry the eggs when the penguins move

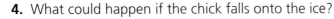

▲ **Emperor penguin chicks grow quickly, so they need a lot of food.**

INFERENCE

4. What could happen if the chick falls onto the ice?

a. Another penguin might take the chick.
b. The chick might die because of the cold.
c. The ice could break and the chick will fall into the water.

DETAIL

5. At what age do most penguin chicks start to live on their own?

a. five months
b. nine months
c. twelve months

SUMMARIZING

B. Complete the summary using the words and phrases in the box (a–f).

a. lays an egg	b. take turns caring for the chick	c. enters the water
d. takes care of the egg	e. move away from the sea	f. hatches

May	The weather gets cold, and the penguins ¹_____. The mother penguin ²_____.
June–July	The father penguin ³_____ through winter.
August	The baby ⁴_____.
August–November	The penguin parents ⁵_____.
December	The chick can live on its own. It ⁶_____ for the first time.

Dealing with New Vocabulary (2)—Using Context

When you find a new word, look at the context—the words around it. This may help you guess its meaning. First, identify the word's part of speech (noun, verb, adjective, adverb, etc.). Then look at the words around it, and try to guess the meaning.

SCANNING **A.** These words appear in Reading A. Find and circle them.

> **protect**   **rapidly**   **several**   **single**

MATCHING **B.** Use the context to help you understand the meaning of each word. Then match each word with its definition (a–d).

1. protect •   • a. only one
2. single •   • b. very quickly
3. several •   • c. to keep safe
4. rapidly •   • d. not many, but more than two

GUESSING WORDS FROM CONTEXT **C.** Read the paragraph below. Use the context to guess the meaning of the words in **bold**. Match each word with its definition.

Snowy owls live mainly in the Arctic. They have excellent **vision**, which they use to hunt for **prey**, such as rabbits and mice. When hunting, snowy owls fly low to the ground. They **grab** their prey with their large, sharp **claws**.

1. _____ (n) the thin nails on an animal's feet
2. _____ (n) the animals that another animal eats
3. _____ (n) the ability to see
4. _____ (v) to catch or hold

CRITICAL THINKING Categorizing Information

▶ Look back at Reading A. Note the things a mother and father penguin do in the chart below.

What a mother penguin does	What a father penguin does

▶ Do you think the mother or father penguin has the more difficult job? Why?

VOCABULARY PRACTICE

COMPLETION **A.** Complete the information using the words and phrases in the box.

adult	on their own	parents	skin	weigh

- Siberian tigers are the largest tigers in the world. A(n) ¹_____ male can grow to three meters long and can ²_____ as much as 320 kilograms.
- Each tiger has black and orange stripes on its fur. Interestingly, the ³_____ under a tiger's fur is also striped.
- Tigers generally like to live ⁴_____. They leave their ⁵_____ when they are still young.

COMPLETION **B.** Complete the sentences. Circle the correct words.

1. Something might **freeze** if it is very *cold / hot*.
2. You need to be **careful** when you are *driving a car / trying to fall asleep*.
3. When you **enter** someone's house, you go *outside / inside*.

WORD USAGE **C.** In the phrase **on (their) own**, the pronoun changes to match the subject of a sentence. Complete these sentences by circling the correct pronoun.

1. Siberian tigers will care for their cubs until they can hunt on (*his / its / their*) own.
2. Most lions do not live on (*his / her / their*) own. They live in groups.
3. Do you want to work with me, or do you prefer to work on (*my / our / your*) own?

Siberian tigers live in very cold places. Their thick fur keeps them warm.

A. Look at the photos. Which word(s) in the box could describe each animal? Do you think animals really have these feelings?

> **anger**   **confusion**   **happiness**   **surprise**

B. Quickly scan the reading. Underline the names you find. How many are there? Which are pets, and which are humans? Read the passage to check your answers.

∧ A capuchin monkey

∧ Two golden snub-nosed monkeys

∧ A brown-throated sloth

∧ A big brown bat

DO ANIMALS LAUGH?

A We know animals have emotions. They can feel **fear**. We also think they feel love, since they have strong **relationships** with each other. So are animal emotions similar to our own? And do animals have a **sense of humor**?

A Parrot's Joke

B Sally Blanchard's parrot Bongo Marie didn't get along[1] with her other parrot, Paco. **In fact**, Bongo Marie clearly didn't like Paco at all! One day, Blanchard cooked a chicken for dinner. She started to cut the chicken with a knife. "Oh, no! Paco!" Bongo Marie said loudly and **laughed**. Blanchard laughed, too, and said, "That's not Paco." "Oh … no," said Bongo Marie. This time, she sounded disappointed.[2] Then the parrot laughed at her own **joke**.

Yoga Dog

C Jean Donaldson enjoys yoga—and so does her dog Buffy. While Donaldson does yoga, Buffy carefully **places** her toys on Donaldson's body. If a toy falls, Buffy runs to put it back. Does this **behavior** have any real purpose? "She thinks it's hilarious!"[3] says Donaldson.

Animal Laughter

D Can dogs "laugh"? Recent research shows that dogs can tell each other when they want to play. They make a special sound—a kind of "laugh." Psychologist Patricia Simonet recorded the sound. Then she played it back to dogs and studied their behavior. "All the dogs seemed to like the laugh," says Simonet. So do animals have a sense of humor? If laughter is a clue, then perhaps the answer is "yes!"

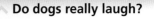
^ Do dogs really laugh?

---

1 When people or animals **get along**, they are friendly and like each other.

2 If someone is **disappointed**, they are sad they didn't get what they wanted.

3 If something is **hilarious**, it is very funny.

A. Choose the best answer for each question.

GIST **1.** What question does the author mainly want to answer?

  a. Do animals have strong relationships?
  b. Do animals have a sense of humor?
  c. Do animals feel love?

DETAIL **2.** What is the purpose of paragraph B?

  a. to explain how parrots can talk
  b. to show how parrots can feel love
  c. to suggest that parrots can make jokes

REFERENCE **3.** In line 4 of paragraph B, the word *She* refers to _____.

  a. Paco
  b. Bongo Marie
  c. Sally Blanchard

⌃ **Some African grey parrots can learn over 500 words and phrases.**

DETAIL **4.** What does Buffy do when Jean Donaldson does yoga?

  a. She tries to jump over Jean.
  b. She copies Jean's movements.
  c. She puts her toys on Jean's body.

MAIN IDEA **5.** What is the main idea of the last paragraph?

  a. Dogs talk to each other, so they seem to be funnier than most animals.
  b. Dogs can make a sound like a laugh, so they may have a sense of humor.
  c. Dogs cannot communicate as well as other animals.

EVALUATING STATEMENTS **B.** Are the following statements true or false, or is the information not given in the passage? Circle **T** (true), **F** (false), or **NG** (not given).

1. Sally Blanchard has a pet dog.   T   F   NG

2. Bongo Marie and Paco are the same type of parrot.   T   F   NG

3. Paco and Bongo Marie are good friends.   T   F   NG

4. Jean Donaldson is a yoga teacher.   T   F   NG

5. Dogs make a special sound when they want to play.   T   F   NG

Identifying Supporting Details

It's important to identify the main idea of a passage. But it's also important to identify details that support that idea. These might include reasons, examples, facts, or descriptions. As you read, ask yourself how well the author supports the main idea of the passage.

ANALYZING **A.** Check (✓) the statements that support the idea "Elephants are very smart animals."

a. ☐ Elephants can live for 60 to 80 years in the wild.

b. ☐ Elephants know themselves when they look in a mirror.

c. ☐ Elephants pull off tree branches and use them to keep flies away.

d. ☐ Elephants live in both Africa and Asia.

e. ☐ Elephants usually have a good sense of humor.

f. ☐ People often kill elephants for their tusks.

An elephant in Zambia reaches for tree branches.

SCANNING **B.** In Reading B, the author suggests that some animals do have a sense of humor. Complete the summary of the supporting details using words from the passage.

Main Idea: It is possible that some animals have a sense of humor.

Supporting Details:

- Sally Blanchard owns two parrots named Bongo Marie and Paco. One day, Bongo Marie told a [1] _____ and then she [2]_____.

- Jean Donaldson's dog Buffy likes to put [3]_____ on Jean's body while she does yoga. If one falls, Buffy puts it back. Jean says that Buffy thinks this is [4]_____.

- Psychologist Patricia Simonet thinks that dogs make a sound that is similar to a human [5]_____. The sound lets other dogs know when they want to [6]_____.

CRITICAL THINKING Evaluating Supporting Details   How well did each example in Reading B support the idea that animals have a sense of humor? Rank the three pieces of supporting evidence in Reading B from 1 (best example) to 3. Explain your ideas to a partner.

_____ A Parrot's Joke   _____ Yoga Dog   _____ Animal Laughter

COMPLETION **A.** Complete the information using the words in the box.

behavior	in fact	placed	relationship

The ¹_____ between apes is often very close. ²_____, they form some of the strongest bonds in the animal kingdom. This was clear when researchers studied a pair of brother and sister bonobos, Kanzi and Panbanisha.

The researchers wanted to see how well the animals had learned to make stone knives. So they gave each bonobo a box with a banana in it. They also gave them the items they needed to make knives, so they could open the boxes.

Kanzi made a good knife, but his sister did not. When he saw that she was sad, Kanzi tried to give his knife to her. When no one was looking, he ³_____ his knife where his sister could find it, and she finally got her banana. Kanzi's ⁴_____ showed how much he cared for his sister.

⌃ **Kanzi the bonobo can make knives from stone, play music, and understand more than 500 English words.**

DEFINITIONS **B.** Complete the sentences. Circle the correct words.

1. When something is *funny* / *sad*, people often **laugh**.

2. Someone is likely to feel **fear** near a *rabbit* / *shark*.

3. A person with a **sense of humor** often says *boring* / *funny* things.

4. A **joke** is something you say to make people *laugh* / *angry*.

WORD FORMS **C.** Many emotions, such as **fear**, can also be described using an adjective. Complete the chart below. Use a dictionary to help.

Emotion (noun)	Adjective(s)
fear	afraid, _____
_____	happy
boredom	_____
_____	angry

A group of narwhals gather in Arctic Bay, Canada.

AMAZING NARWHALS

BEFORE YOU WATCH

PREVIEWING   **A.** Read the information. The words in **bold** appear in the video. Complete the definitions.

They have sometimes been called the "unicorns of the sea," and it's easy to see why. Narwhals are a type of whale. Each one has a **tusk** that grows on its head. The tusk is very **sensitive** and very long. For many years, scientists were not **certain** about the tusk's purpose. However, recent discoveries have provided some useful clues.

1. A person or thing that is _____ to something is easily affected by it.

2. If you are _____ about something, you are sure of it

3. A _____ is a kind of tooth that animals such as elephants have.

DISCUSSION   **B.** What do you think a narwhal's tusk might be used for? Work with a partner and brainstorm some ideas. Note your answers below.

_____

_____

GIST **A.** Watch the video. Which of your ideas in Before You Watch B are mentioned?

SHORT ANSWERS **B.** Watch the video again. Write short answers to the questions.

1. Where do narwhals live?

_____

2. How long can a narwhal's tusk grow?

_____

3. In the past, why did people buy narwhal tusks?

_____

4. What did researchers see narwhals doing in 2017?

_____

CRITICAL THINKING Applying Ideas

▶ Why do you think its difficult for researchers to study narwhals? Note some ideas below. Then discuss with a partner.

_____

_____

▶ What other kinds of animals might be difficult to study? Discuss with a partner.

VOCABULARY REVIEW

Do you remember the meanings of these words and phrases? Check (✓) the ones you know. Look back at the unit and review any you're not sure of.

Reading A

☐ adult*   ☐ careful   ☐ enter   ☐ freeze

☐ on your own ☐ parent   ☐ skin   ☐ weigh

Reading B

☐ behavior   ☐ fear   ☐ in fact   ☐ joke

☐ laugh   ☐ place   ☐ relationship ☐ sense of humor

* Academic Word List

BUILDING
BEAUTY

9

The Sheikh Zayed Grand
Mosque, Abu Dhabi, U.A.E.

WARM UP

Discuss these questions
with a partner.

1. What do you think is the
   most interesting thing
   about this building?

2. What is the most famous
   building in your country?
   Why?

BEFORE YOU READ

DEFINITIONS **A.** Look at the photo and read the caption. Match each word in **bold** with its definition.

1. _____: the male ruler of an empire
2. _____: a type of stone often used in buildings
3. _____: large structures built to remind people of a famous event or person

PREVIEWING **B.** Why do you think Shah Jahan built the Taj Mahal? Read the passage to check your ideas.

> The Taj Mahal in Agra, India, is one of the most famous **monuments** in the world. The **emperor** Shah Jahan built the Taj Mahal from white **marble**.

A LOVE POEM IN STONE

A Often called "a love poem[1] in stone," the Taj Mahal is one of the most beautiful buildings ever made. It is also perhaps the most beautiful expression[2] of love in the world.

B The emperor Shah Jahan built the Taj Mahal for his empress, Mumtaz Mahal. They lived happily **together** for 18 years. Then, in 1631, Mumtaz died **during** the **birth** of their fourteenth child. Before she died, the emperor made her a **promise**. To remember her, he would build the most beautiful monument in the world.

C Building the Taj Mahal was a huge task. It is said that it took more than 20,000 people and 1,000 elephants. They worked for over 20 years to build the monument and its **central** dome.[3]

D In 1658, five years after the building was **finished**, Shah Jahan's son became emperor. He put Shah Jahan in prison.[4] Shah Jahan stayed there until his death in 1666. His body was then put in the Taj Mahal with the woman he loved.

▲ **A painting of Shah Jahan and Mumtaz Mahal**

E There are many legends about the Taj Mahal. In one story, Shah Jahan had the builders' hands cut off after the building was **complete**. This was supposedly done so they could never build anything as beautiful as the Taj Mahal. Another says he also wanted to build a black Taj Mahal. These are interesting stories, but they are probably not true.

F The love story between Shah Jahan and his wife ended sadly. But the monument to their love still stands today. Millions of **tourists** visit every year. They come to see the marble change color in the light of the rising sun or a full moon.

---

1 A **poem** is a piece of writing that usually has rhythm.

2 An **expression** of love is a way of showing your feelings.

3 A **dome** is a rounded roof.

4 A **prison** is a place where people who break the law are kept.

A. Choose the best answer for each question.

GIST

1. What could be another title for the reading?

   a. The Emperor and Empress's Home
   b. How an Emperor Showed His Love
   c. The Beautiful Writings of Shah Jahan

PARAPHRASING

2. What is another way of saying *It is said that* (paragraph C)?

   a. It is true that
   b. We said that
   c. Some people believe that

REFERENCE

3. In the second sentence of paragraph D, who does the word *He* refer to?

   a. Shah Jahan
   b. Shah Jahan's son
   c. Shah Jahan's father

DETAIL

4. Which of these statements about the Taj Mahal is true?

   a. It took more than 20 years to build.
   b. Shah Jahan died inside it in 1666.
   c. Its central dome was never completed.

∧ **The interior of the Taj Mahal is decorated with a number of detailed carvings.**

MAIN IDEA

5. What is the main idea of paragraph F?

   a. The best time to visit the Taj Mahal is in the early morning.
   b. Today, the Taj Mahal continues to express Shah Jahan's love.
   c. The Taj Mahal looks very different from modern buildings.

CREATING A TIMELINE

Review this reading skill in Unit 6A

B. Complete the timeline with the events in the box (a–f).

   a. Shah Jahan's son put his father in prison.
   b. The Taj Mahal was completed.
   c. Shah Jahan's son became emperor.
   d. Shah Jahan made Mumtaz Mahal a promise.
   e. Mumtaz Mahal died.
   f. Shah Jahan died.

1631   1653   1658   1666

Annotating Text

As you read, it can be useful to annotate—or mark up—the text. This way you can identify the most important information so you can remember it later. Here are some ways to add annotations.

- Highlight the main ideas or most important parts.
- Put a circle around important numbers or dates.
- Underline new words and write their definitions in the margins.
- Put a question mark (?) next to things you don't understand, for checking later.

ANNOTATING **A.** Look at these two annotated paragraphs from "A Love Poem in Stone." Then annotate the rest of Reading A.

empress = emperor's wife

The emperor Shah Jahan built the Taj Mahal for his empress, Mumtaz Mahal. They lived happily together for 18 years. Then, in 1631, Mumtaz died during the birth of their fourteenth child. Before she died, the emperor made her a promise. To remember her, he would build the most beautiful monument in the world.

dome = rounded roof

?

Building the Taj Mahal was a huge task. It is said that it took more than 20,000 people and 1,000 elephants. They worked for over 20 years to build the monument and its central dome.

SUMMARIZING **B.** Look back at your annotated text in Reading A. Then complete the concept map below with words and numbers from the reading.

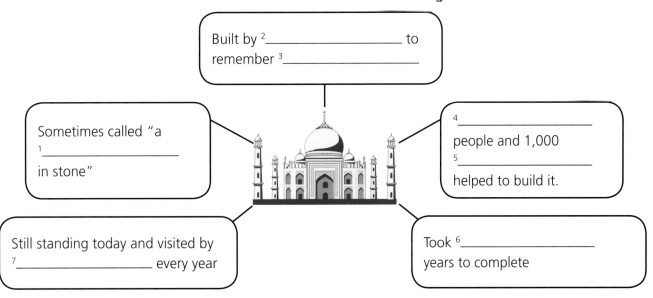

Built by 2_____ to
remember 3_____

Sometimes called "a
1_____
in stone"

4_____
people and 1,000
5_____
helped to build it.

Still standing today and visited by
7_____ every year

Took 6_____
years to complete

CRITICAL THINKING Understanding Opinions   Discuss with a partner. What two legends about the Taj Mahal are mentioned in the reading? What is the author's opinion about these legends?

COMPLETION   **A.** Complete the information using the words in the box. One word is extra.

during	finished	promises	together	tourists

Millions of ¹_____ visit the Taj Mahal every year. Most know the story behind the white marble monument, but few know the legend of the black Taj Mahal.

Today, the bodies of Shah Jahan and Mumtaz Mahal lie ²_____ inside the Taj Mahal. However, according to the legend, after Shah Jahan ³_____ the Taj Mahal, he actually wanted his own monument. It would be across the river from the Taj Mahal, but made from black marble instead of white.

⁴_____ the 1990s, archeologists searched the area and found pieces of black stone. However, a closer look showed that these were just white stones that had turned black. Today, there is still no real proof that the story is true.

∧ **Some think the reflection of the Taj Mahal at sunset may have started the story of the black Taj Mahal.**

DEFINITIONS   **B.** Complete the sentences. Circle the correct options.

1. If a building is **complete**, there is *no more / a lot more* work to be done on it.

2. When you make a **promise**, you tell someone that you *need to / will* do something.

3. Something that is **central** is *at the side / in the middle* of a place or area.

4. The **birth** of a person is the time he or she *dies / is born*.

COLLOCATIONS   **C.** The verbs in the box are often used with the noun **promise**. Complete the sentences using the correct words.

break	keep	make

1. Don't _____ a promise if you don't think you can do it.

2. A true friend would never _____ a promise.

3. I said I would help you. I always _____ my promises.

BEFORE YOU READ

PREDICTING

A. Look at the picture and read the caption. Then discuss the questions below with a partner.

    1. What do you think the building's dome is made of?

    2. Why do you think it took so long to complete the dome?

SKIMMING

B. Skim the reading and check your ideas in activity A.

Today, the Basilica di Santa Maria del Fiore is one of Florence's greatest sights. The building of the cathedral began in 1296. The dome, however, was not finished until 140 years later.

THE GREAT DOME OF FLORENCE

St. Peter's Basilica
Vatican City
1626

Santa Maria del Fiore
Florence, Italy
1471

St. Paul's Cathedral
London, England
1710

U.S. Capitol
Washington, D.C., U.S.
1868

Gol Gumbad
Bijapur, India
ca 1656

Taj Mahal
Agra, India
ca 1653

Hagia Sophia
Istanbul, Turkey
537

Pantheon
Rome, Italy
ca 130

A   In 1419, a clockmaker named Filippo Brunelleschi started work on a very difficult project. He was building the dome of Florence's main cathedral,[1] the Basilica di Santa Maria del Fiore. For 1,500 years, the world's largest dome belonged to the Pantheon in Rome. Brunelleschi's job was to build one even larger.

B   The building of the cathedral began in 1296. By 1359, much of it was complete, but no one knew how to build its dome. Many builders could build concrete[2] domes. However, the dome in Florence needed to be **wider** than any dome ever built. A concrete dome would be too heavy and would easily fall. The cathedral, therefore, **remained** unfinished for many years.

C   Filippo Brunelleschi promised to find a **solution**. He said he would build *two* domes, an inner dome made of stone and an outer one made of **light** bricks.[3] He would use lighter materials as he worked upwards. Strong rings made of stone, wood, and iron would hold everything together.

D   Brunelleschi also had to find a way to **lift** the materials high into the air. What did he do? He **invented** a new machine to do the job.

E   Building the dome took 16 years. Brunelleschi had done something no one else could. However, he left no pictures of his **design**. So—even today—experts don't fully understand how this **incredible** structure was built.

> **The dome in Florence is second in size only to St. Peter's Basilica in Vatican City.**

---

1 A **cathedral** is a kind of church building, usually quite big and beautiful.
2 **Concrete** is a hard material, similar to stone.
3 **Bricks** are small pieces of hard material used for building.

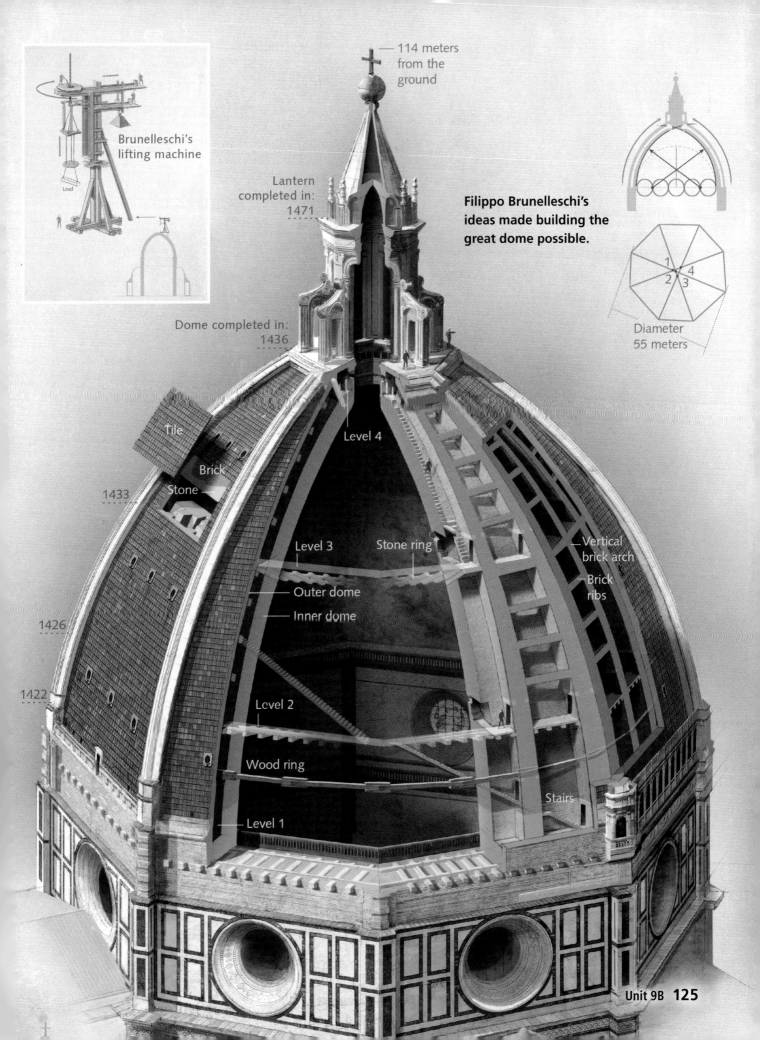

114 meters from the ground

Brunelleschi's lifting machine

Load

Lantern completed in: 1471

Filippo Brunelleschi's ideas made building the great dome possible.

1 4
2 3

Diameter 55 meters

Dome completed in: 1436

Tile

Brick

Stone

1433

Level 4

Level 3

Stone ring

Outer dome

Inner dome

Vertical brick arch

Brick ribs

1426

1422

Level 2

Wood ring

Stairs

Level 1

A. Choose the best answer for each question.

DETAIL

1. Which of the following is NOT given as a reason the dome was difficult to build?

    a. No one had ever built a dome from concrete before.

    b. No one had built such a wide dome before.

    c. Materials needed to be lifted high into the air.

PURPOSE

2. What is the purpose of paragraph C?

    a. to argue another side of an issue

    b. to explain a solution to a problem

    c. to provide background information

DETAIL

3. What is NOT true about Filippo Brunelleschi?

    a. He built two domes for the cathedral.

    b. He wanted to build the dome using only one material.

    c. He invented a machine that lifted things into the air.

△ **The Florence cathedral is just as impressive from the inside.**

COHESION

4. The following sentence would best be placed at the end of which paragraph?

As a result, there was a large hole in the cathedral's roof.

    a. paragraph A   b. paragraph B   c. paragraph C

DETAIL

5. Why don't we fully understand how the dome was built?

    a. Brunelleschi didn't leave any pictures of his design.

    b. It is covered in concrete and therefore difficult to study.

    c. The dome has been rebuilt many times over the years.

IDENTIFYING MAIN IDEAS

Review this reading skill in Unit 4A

B. Match the paragraphs with the best heading in the box (a–e). One heading is extra.

a. Problem Solved	b. A Great Achievement	c. A New Invention
d. Cathedral Without a Dome	e. The Cathedral Today	

1. _____ Paragraph B

2. _____ Paragraph C

3. _____ Paragraph D

4. _____ Paragraph E

Understanding Infographics

An information graphic (infographic) uses text and images to present information. It may show many kinds of information such as text, photos, illustrations, maps, labels, captions, charts, and graphs. Look for keys and other clues—such as colors—to help you fully understand the information.

UNDERSTANDING INFOGRAPHICS

A. What information does the infographic on page 125 show? Check (✓) all that are true.

☐ how materials were lifted to the top of the cathedral

☐ the shape of the dome when viewed from above

☐ what the cathedral looked like before the dome was finished

☐ the different materials used to build the dome

UNDERSTANDING INFOGRAPHICS

B. Complete the sentences below about the infographic on page 125.

1. There are *three / four* levels in the dome.

2. The dome has *six / eight* sides.

3. The outside of the dome is covered in *bricks / tiles*.

4. A *stone / wood* ring is below Level 2.

5. Level *three / four* was finished by 1433.

UNDERSTANDING INFOGRAPHICS

C. Look back at the infographic on page 124. Note answers to the questions.

1. Which building has the biggest dome? _____

2. Which building is the oldest? _____

CRITICAL THINKING Synthesizing Information

▶ Use information from Reading A and Reading B to complete the chart comparing the Basilica di Santa Maria del Fiore with the Taj Mahal.

Building name:	Taj Mahal	Santa Maria del Fiore
Location:	1_____	5_____
Construction began:	2_____	6_____
Completed:	3_____	1471
Material(s) used:	mainly 4_____	wood, stone, bricks, iron
Width of dome:	28 meters	55 meters
Height of building:	73 meters	115 meters

▶ Which building do you think was the greatest achievement? Discuss with a partner. Use information from the box above and your own ideas to support your opinion.

VOCABULARY PRACTICE

COMPLETION **A.** Complete the information using the correct words in the box.

| design   incredible   light   remains   wide |

The O2 Arena, or simply "The Dome," is a stadium for music and sporting events in London, United Kingdom. At around 365 meters ¹_____ and 52 meters high, the dome is a huge structure. However, the material used to build the dome itself is only a millimeter thick. This makes it very ²_____. The air inside the dome is heavier than the roof.

Completed in 2000, it was first known as the Millennium Dome. While some were excited by the interesting and modern ³_____, others were unhappy at its ⁴_____ cost. Some suggest the total amount of money spent on building the dome was around 700 million pounds—enough to build many hospitals. Today, however, it ⁵_____ a popular place to visit in London.

∧ **The O2 Arena is 52 meters tall, each meter representing one week of the year.**

DEFINITIONS **B.** Complete the sentences. Circle the correct words.

1. If you **invent** something, you are the first person to *make / use* it.

2. When you **lift** something, you move it to a *higher / lower* place.

3. A **solution** is the *answer to / cause of* a problem.

WORD FORMS **C.** Some words, like **design**, can act as nouns and verbs.

Example: The stadium's **design** is incredible. I want to **design** tall buildings like that.

Write two sentences for each word, one as a noun and one as a verb.

promise:_____
_____

laugh: _____
_____

trust: _____
_____

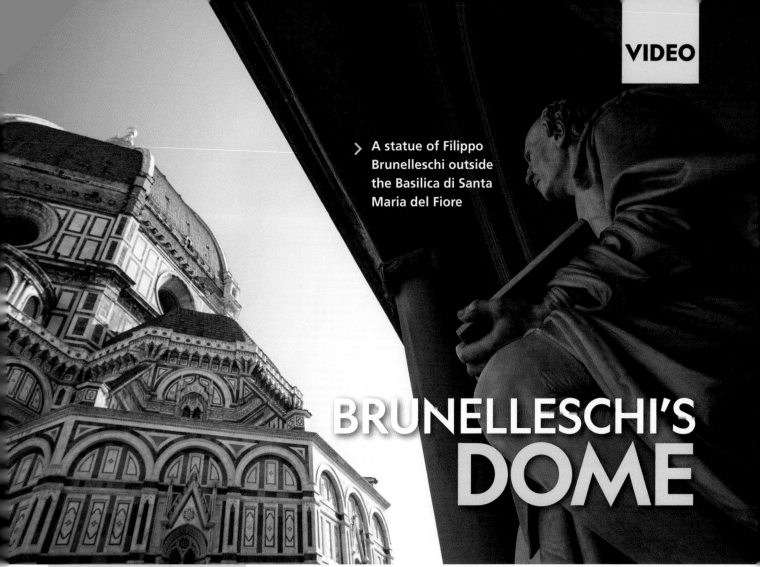

> A statue of Filippo Brunelleschi outside the Basilica di Santa Maria del Fiore

BRUNELLESCHI'S DOME

BEFORE YOU WATCH

PREVIEWING **A.** Read the extracts from the video. Match each word in **bold** with the correct picture.

"At the time, domes were often built as **semicircles**."

"The bottom of the dome was shaped like an **octagon**."

"The domes would be held together by giant brick **arches**."

1. _____

2. _____

3. _____

QUIZ **B.** What do you remember about Filippo Brunelleschi and the Santa Maria del Fiore? Answer the questions.

1. Where is the Santa Maria del Fiore?
2. What was Brunelleschi's job before he started work on the dome?
3. In which century was the dome of the Santa Maria del Fiore completed?
4. How were heavy materials moved to the top of the dome?

GIST **A.** Watch the video. Check your answers in Before You Watch B.

DETAILS **B.** Watch the video again. Complete the sentences by circling the correct options.

1. Brunelleschi accepted the job because _____.
   a. he loved beautiful buildings
   b. he was given a lot of money

2. The dome was difficult to build because _____.
   a. it had eight sides
   b. it was a semicircle

3. Brunelleschi built two domes because he _____.
   a. wanted to try different designs
   b. needed to make the structure strong

4. Brick arches and rings of stone and wood were used _____.
   a. to carry materials to the roof
   b. to hold the domes together

5. Brunelleschi used a special pattern of bricks so that _____.
   a. the dome would look beautiful
   b. they would hold together

CRITICAL THINKING Inferring Information   Brunelleschi wasn't trained as an architect, but he was an expert clockmaker. How do you think his clock-making skills helped him design and build the dome? Note your ideas below. Then discuss with a partner.

_____

_____

_____

VOCABULARY REVIEW

Do you remember the meanings of these words? Check (✓) the ones you know. Look back at the unit and review any words you're not sure of.

Reading A

☐ birth   ☐ central   ☐ complete   ☐ during

☐ finish   ☐ promise   ☐ together   ☐ tourist

Reading B

☐ design*   ☐ incredible   ☐ invent   ☐ lift

☐ light   ☐ remain   ☐ solution   ☐ wide

*Academic Word List

10

FORCES OF NATURE

Huge waves crash against the
Mouro Island lighthouse in Spain.

WARM UP

Discuss these questions with a partner.

1. What's the weather usually like where
   you live? Have you experienced any wild
   weather in your country?

2. Do you think humans are able to cause
   changes in the weather?

131

10A

DEFINITIONS

Review this reading skill in Unit 3A

A. Scan paragraph B of the reading passage. Circle the nouns that describe different types of wild weather. Check the meaning of each one in a dictionary.

SKIMMING

B. Skim the reading passage on the next two pages. What is it mainly about? Circle **a**, **b**, or **c**. Then read the passage to check your answer.

  a. why the United States is getting more dangerous storms
  b. how scientists are able to predict the weather
  c. how the weather is changing around the world

> **Areas along the Kamo River in Kyoto, Japan, were affected by heavy flooding in July 2018.**

WILD WEATHER

A In late June 2018, the weather **forecast** for western Japan predicted heavy rain, but no one was prepared for what was to come. By mid-July, **large** areas were flooded. Some areas received over 100 centimeters of rain. Cars and trucks **floated** down the streets. Whole buildings were washed away. **At least** 225 people died, and millions had to leave their homes.

Changing Weather

B The weather is changing. Over the last few years, heavy rains have caused floods in many parts of the world. There have been droughts in Brazil and Australia. Heat waves in Europe have killed thousands. There have been more hurricanes and tornadoes, and they have struck with more **power** than ever before. In 2017 alone, the **financial** cost from weather events around the world was 340 billion dollars.

Warmer and Wetter

C As more wild weather events happen, people are asking questions: What is happening with the weather? And why? Is this natural, or are we to **blame**?

D The answer seems to be: *a little of both*. Wild weather is natural. But most scientists agree human activity has made the Earth warmer. This global warming makes heat waves more likely. The higher **temperatures** also cause more water to enter the air. This causes heavier and more frequent rain. Many scientists also believe global warming makes hurricanes and other storms stronger.

E This means we're likely to see more wild weather. "[But] we don't have to just stand there and take it," says scientist Michael Oppenheimer. He and other experts say we need to stop the Earth from getting warmer. We also need to be prepared, to do things that will help save lives.

Trees bend as Hurricane Irma hits Florida, United States, in 2017.

A. Choose the best answer for each question.

MAIN IDEA
1. What is the main idea of the reading passage?

   a. There was a deadly flood in Japan.

   b. Global warming is causing wilder weather events.

   c. In 2011, there were many wild weather events.

PURPOSE
2. What is the purpose of paragraph B?

   a. to give examples of recent wild weather events

   b. to describe a serious flood that happened in 2017

   c. to predict how the weather will change in a few years

REFERENCE
3. In paragraph C, what does *this* refer to?

   a. a worried world

   b. the increase in wild weather

   c. deaths caused by wild weather

Lightning can heat the air around it to five times the temperature of the sun.

MAIN IDEA
4. What is the main idea of paragraph D?

   a. Scientists are trying to understand what causes hurricanes.

   b. Wild weather is partly a result of human activity.

   c. Higher temperatures lead to more rainfall.

INFERENCE
5. Which of the following statements would Oppenheimer probably agree with?

   a. It is too late to stop global warming.

   b. Stop global warming, and the weather will get better.

   c. Extreme weather is not caused by global warming.

SCANNING
Review this reading skill in Unit 1A

B. Write short answers to the questions below. Use one to three words from the passage for each answer.

1. How much rain fell in some areas of Japan in July 2018?

2. Which two countries are given as examples of places that experienced droughts?

3. What causes more water to enter the air?

4. Which scientist is quoted in paragraph E?

Understanding Tenses

Understanding the different tenses used by a writer is an important part of reading comprehension. Different tenses carry different meanings. For example:

- **Simple present** is used to describe facts.

  Melting ice sometimes <u>causes</u> flooding.

- **Present continuous** is used to describe changing situations.

  Global temperatures <u>are increasing</u> every year.

- **Simple past** is used to describe finished past events.

  In 2015, there <u>was</u> a terrible drought in my hometown.

- **Present perfect** is used to describe recent or unfinished events.

  In recent years, floods <u>have affected</u> many parts of England.

UNDERSTANDING TENSES

A. Look back at paragraphs A, B, and D in Reading A. What does each paragraph describe? Match the sentence halves.

1. Paragraph A •
2. Paragraph B •
3. Paragraph D •

- a. describes a past weather event.
- b. describes facts about global warming.
- c. describes a number of recent weather events.

UNDERSTANDING TENSES

B. In each paragraph (A, B, and D), find and underline all the verbs. Which tense is mainly used in each paragraph? Note your answers below.

Paragraph A: _____

Paragraph B: _____

Paragraph D: _____

UNDERSTANDING TENSES

C. Scan the reading again. Find two present continuous sentences. What changing situation do they describe?

UNDERSTANDING TENSES

D. Now look back at the reading passages below. What tense is mainly used in each one? Why? Note your answers.

Reading 5A, *The Disease Detective*: _____

Reading 8A, *A Penguin's Year*: _____

CRITICAL THINKING Personalizing   Think of a wild weather event that happened in your country. Make notes about it below. Then describe the event to your partner.

What was the weather event? _____

When and where did it happen? _____

How did it affect people? _____

COMPLETION **A.** Complete the information using the words in the box. One is extra.

> at least financial float forecasts large temperatures

In recent years, Australia has seen a lot of wild weather. In 2018, heat waves affected much of the country, with ¹_____ in some places nearing 50 degrees Celsius. In the same year, forest fires destroyed ²_____ areas of land. In early 2019—after years of drought—Queensland suffered from heavy flooding.

The ³_____ cost of these weather events is huge. Estimates suggest that over the last 10 years, damage from wild weather has cost Australia ⁴_____ 25 billion dollars. Because of this, more scientists are studying its weather patterns to see if they can help make better weather ⁵_____.

∧ **Firefighters in Queensland battle a forest fire.**

DEFINITIONS **B.** Complete the sentences. Choose the correct words.

1. An example of something that **floats** is _____.
   a. a rock   b. a piece of wood

2. A _____ has a lot of **power**.
   a. flower   b. tornado

3. If you **blame** someone, you say they _____.
   a. caused something bad to happen
   b. stopped something bad from happening

WORD PARTS **C.** As in **forecast**, the prefix *fore-* means "at the front" or "before." Complete the sentences using the words in the box.

> forecast foreground forehead foresight

1. I'm glad you had the _____ to prepare for the hurricane.
2. Her head hurt, so she put a cool towel across her _____.
3. According to the weather _____, we will have clear skies tonight.
4. The flowers in the _____ of this photo look beautiful.

BEFORE YOU READ

DISCUSSION **A.** Look at the photo and read the caption. Then discuss these questions with a partner.

    1. What other strange weather events have you heard of? Can you explain why they happen?

    2. Do you know any interesting stories about strange weather?

SKIMMING **B.** Quickly skim the reading passage. Match the headings below to the correct paragraphs in the passage. One heading is extra.

    a. Tornadoes of Fire   c. Huge Hail

    b. Rising Floods   d. Strange Rain

> ∨ A giant cloud of dust, called a *haboob*, covers the city of Phoenix, Arizona, USA. The wall of dust is 1,500 meters tall and 160 kilometers long.

WHEN WEIRD WEATHER STRIKES

A Most of us know about hurricanes, droughts, and floods. But from time to time, nature **delivers** a weather event that is really **unusual**.

1 _____

B One day in 2005, people in a small town in Serbia saw an unusual sight. It was raining frogs! Without any **warning**, they found their streets filling with the little jumping creatures. "There were thousands of them," one person told a **local** newspaper. "I thought perhaps a plane carrying frogs had **exploded**," said another. Scientists believe a tornado passed over a lake and sucked up the frogs. It then **dropped** them on the town, far away.

2 _____

C As if tornadoes aren't dangerous enough, some can **actually** be made of fire. When a wildfire reaches very high temperatures, it causes the air to heat up and then rise. Cooler air moves quickly to replace the hot air. This creates strong winds, which suck up the fire. When this happens—like it did in 2014, in Denver, United States—a fire tornado is created. A tornado like this can become 15 meters wide and grow as tall as a 40-story building.

3 _____

D In 1942, hundreds of thousand-year-old skeletons were found under the ice of Lake Roopkund in the Himalayas. Many had holes in their skulls—but they weren't hurt in any other way. For years, the cause of their deaths was a mystery. Today, scientists think they were killed by giant hailstones. Hailstones are balls of ice that form when raindrops turn into ice. The ice pieces **increase** in size until the wind cannot hold them up. This results in hailstones falling to the ground, often at speeds of over 160 kilometers an hour. For the unlucky people at Lake Roopkund, there was nowhere to run.

> ∧ A tornado of fire is formed by strong winds in a forest fire.

A. Choose the best answer for each question.

PURPOSE

1. What is the main purpose of the reading?

   a. to explain some new research into wild weather
   b. to describe some ways to prepare for unusual weather
   c. to give examples of strange weather

VOCABULARY

2. In paragraph B, the phrase *sucked up* could be replaced with _____.

   a. lifted
   b. used
   c. blew

∧ **Some hailstones can be as large as tennis balls.**

DETAIL

3. What is probably true about the frogs that rained down in Serbia?

   a. They fell out of an airplane.
   b. They were dropped by a tornado.
   c. They fell from very tall trees.

DETAIL

4. What causes fire tornadoes?

   a. extremely hot wildfires
   b. house fires in windy weather
   c. fires in very tall buildings

DETAIL

5. What is NOT true about the skeletons found at Lake Roopkund?

   a. They were discovered in 1942.
   b. They were thousands of years old.
   c. They showed no signs of injury.

MATCHING

B. **Which sentence could be placed at the end of each paragraph? Match each paragraph to a sentence. One sentence is extra.**

   1. Paragraph A _____   a. Sadly, they were all killed that day.

   2. Paragraph B _____   b. This likely caused a large flood.

   3. Paragraph C _____   c. It is one of nature's most terrifying creations.

   4. Paragraph D _____   d. Here are some examples of truly weird weather.

                                 e. Surprisingly, many survived the fall to the ground.

READING SKILL

Understanding Cause and Effect

A *cause* is an action that makes something happen. An *effect* is a result of the action. To fully understand a reading, it's important to notice how ideas connect in this way.

To identify causes and effects, you can often look out for words like *cause*, *result*, *create*, and *make*. However, causes and effects are sometimes described without using these words. When two events in a passage seem to be connected, ask yourself: *Which event occurred first? Did it change the event that follows?*

SCANNING **A.** Look back at Reading B. Find examples of causes and effects in the passage. Underline the causes and circle the effects.

MATCHING **B.** Match the causes on the left with the effects on the right.

Causes	Effects
1. a tornado passes over a lake •	• a. hail falls to the ground
2. a wildfire reaches high temperatures •	• b. strong winds are created
3. cool air rushes into a wildfire •	• c. the air becomes hot and rises
4. wildfire winds suck up the fire itself •	• d. frogs are lifted into the air
5. pieces of ice in the air grow too big •	• e. a tornado of fire is produced

UNDERSTANDING CAUSE AND EFFECT **C.** Now look back at Reading A, paragraph D. Complete the chart below with the causes and effects.

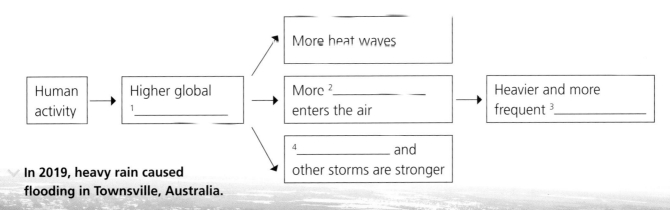

Human activity → Higher global ^{1}_____ →

More heat waves

More ^{2}_____ enters the air → Heavier and more frequent ^{3}_____

^{4}_____ and other storms are stronger

In 2019, heavy rain caused flooding in Townsville, Australia.

COMPLETION **A.** Complete the information using the words in the box. One word is extra.

actually	increase	local	unusual	warning

Mystery Waves

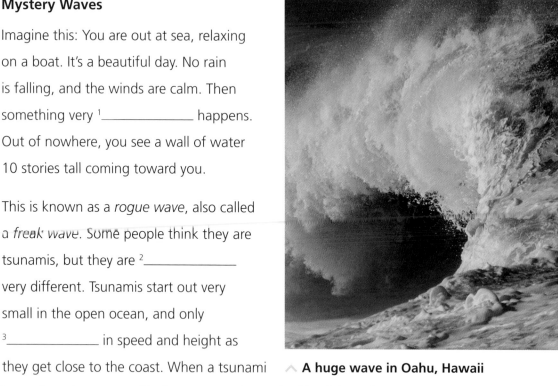

▲ **A huge wave in Oahu, Hawaii**

Imagine this: You are out at sea, relaxing on a boat. It's a beautiful day. No rain is falling, and the winds are calm. Then something very ¹_____ happens. Out of nowhere, you see a wall of water 10 stories tall coming toward you.

This is known as a *rogue wave*, also called a *freak wave*. Some people think they are tsunamis, but they are ²_____ very different. Tsunamis start out very small in the open ocean, and only ³_____ in speed and height as they get close to the coast. When a tsunami is coming, the water will often seem to be sucked back into the ocean. However, there is usually no ⁴_____ before a rogue wave strikes.

Scientists aren't sure what causes these waves. But they know they are very real—and very dangerous—even to the largest ships.

DEFINITIONS **B.** Match each word in **red** with its definition.

1. If you **drop** something, •   • a. you take it and give it to someone.
2. If a place is **local**, •   • b. it suddenly breaks into many pieces.
3. If something **explodes**, •   • c. it is not far away.
4. If you **deliver** something, •   • d. it falls to the ground.

WORD WEB **C.** Complete the chart with synonyms (similar words) and antonyms (opposite words) of **unusual**. Use a dictionary to help.

synonyms: ¹ o _ _   ² w _ _ _ _   ³ s _ _ _ _ _ _

antonyms: ⁴ u _ _ _ _   ⁵ n _ _ _ _ _   ⁶ o _ _ _ _ _ _ y

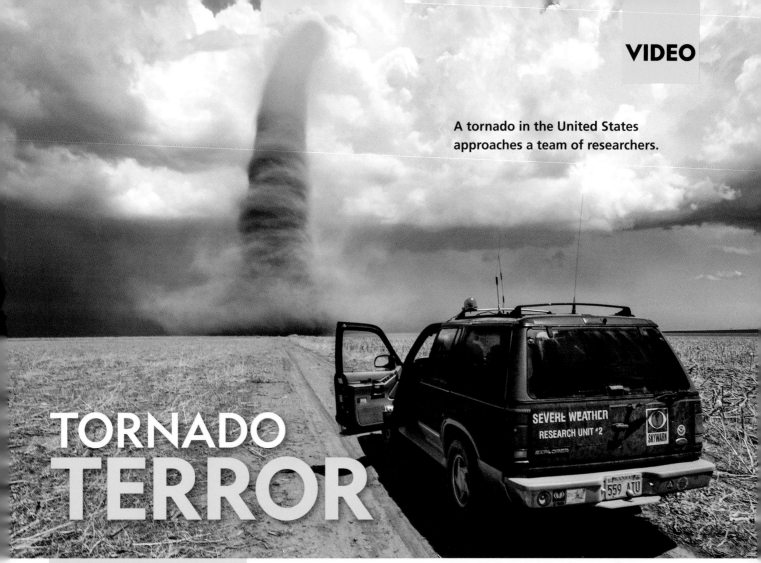

A tornado in the United States approaches a team of researchers.

TORNADO TERROR

BEFORE YOU WATCH

PREVIEWING **A.** Read the information. The words and phrases in **bold** appear in the video. Match each word with its definition.

Every year, the United States experiences an **average** of 1,000 tornadoes. This happens when warm wet air meets cold dry air in a thunderstorm. A tall cloud of **spinning** wind is **formed**. When it touches the ground, it becomes a tornado. Tornadoes can be deadly. Some are strong enough to pick up whole houses.

1. When something is _____, it is created or takes shape.

2. If something is described as _____, it is ordinary or usual.

3. If something is _____, it is turning very quickly.

QUIZ **B.** What do you know about tornadoes? Read the sentences below. Circle **T** (true) or **F** (false).

1. Tornadoes are sometimes called "twisters." T F

2. Most of the world's tornadoes happen in the United States. T F

3. Some tornadoes are more than one kilometer wide. T F

4. Tornadoes occur on every continent in the world. T F

GIST **A.** Watch the video. Check your answers in Before You Watch B.

DETAILS **B.** Watch the video again. Complete the sentences using the numbers (a–e) in the box.

a. 13	b. 60	c. 75	d. 170	e. 1,300

1. Tornadoes can travel at speeds of around _____ km/h.
2. Almost _____ percent of the world's tornadoes happen in the United States.
3. On average, a tornado warning only gives people _____ minutes to find safety.
4. In the United States, _____ people are killed by tornadoes each year.
5. In Dhaka, Bangladesh, a single tornado killed around _____ people.

CRITICAL THINKING Ranking Advice   Imagine your car is stuck in traffic, and a huge tornado is coming your way. What do you think is the best thing to do? Rank the pieces of advice below from 1–4 (1 = best advice). Compare your answers with a partner and explain your reasons.

a. Stay in your car, open all the windows, and put your seatbelt on. _____
b. Stay in your car, lock all the doors, and lie down on the back seat. _____
c. Get out of your car, move far away from it, and lie flat on the ground. _____
d. Get out of your car and hide underneath it until the storm passes. _____

VOCABULARY REVIEW

Do you remember the meanings of these words? Check (✓) the ones you know. Look back at the unit and review any words you're not sure of.

Reading A

☐ at least   ☐ blame   ☐ financial*   ☐ float

☐ forecast   ☐ large   ☐ power   ☐ temperature

Reading B

☐ actually   ☐ deliver   ☐ drop   ☐ explode

☐ increase   ☐ local   ☐ unusual   ☐ warning

*Academic Word List

11

GIANTS OF
THE PAST

Millions of years ago, super-sized creatures like the dinosaurs walked the Earth and swam the seas.

WARM UP

Discuss these questions with a partner.

1. Do you know of any animals that don't exist anymore?

2. What do you think caused these animals to die out?

11A

BEFORE YOU READ

PREVIEWING **A.** Tens of thousands of years ago, woolly mammoths walked the Earth. These creatures were related to today's elephants. Read the information below. Then match the words in **bold** to their definitions.

MAMMOTH

- Long, thick hair
- Long, curved **tusks**
- Lived during the **Ice Age** in Siberia and North America
- Became **extinct** 4,000 years ago

ELEPHANT

- Thick skin but very little hair
- Short, straight tusks
- 470,000 living today, mainly in hot places like India and Africa

1. _____: no longer living

2. _____: a time when the Earth was very cold

3. _____: long, pointed teeth used to fight or to find food

PREDICTING **B.** Look at the pictures and captions on this page and the next. What do you think happened to the mammoth after it was found? Discuss with a partner. Then read the passage to check your ideas.

Lyuba is the best-preserved mammoth mummy in the world.

THE MAMMOTH'S TALE

A   The strange animal in the ice looked like it was sleeping. Ten-year-old Kostia Khudi and his brother had never seen anything like it. Their father, a reindeer herder[1] named Yuri Khudi, went to ask a friend for advice. But when he returned, the body had **disappeared**.

B   Yuri soon found the animal's body leaning against a **store** in a **nearby** town. While he was away, his cousin had sold it to the store **owner**. Dogs had eaten part of the tail and ear. But it was still in almost "as close to **perfect** condition as you can **imagine**," says scientist Daniel Fisher. The police came to help. The body was taken by helicopter to a museum. The animal was a baby mammoth from the Ice Age. It was female, so the scientists named it after Yuri's wife.

C   From Siberia, the mammoth was sent to the Netherlands and Japan. Scientists there studied it **in detail**. Studies of her teeth and tusks showed she was just one month old when she died. Research has also shown us the sequence of events that led to her death. Lyuba fell and died near a muddy river. The mud[2] helped keep her body frozen until she was found, 40,000 years later. Scientists hope that **further** studies will help explain how mammoths like Lyuba lived. They also want to know why mammoths became extinct.

1 A **herder** looks after a large group of animals.
2 **Mud** is a wet sticky mix of earth and water.

Lyuba died when she fell into wet mud near a river.

The ground froze. It kept Lyuba's body whole.

In 2006, melting caused Lyuba's body to wash free.

A. Choose the best answer for each question.

GIST 1. The passage is mainly about _____.

a. why mammoths became extinct
b. an important discovery
c. what life was like for a mammoth named Lyuba

DETAIL 2. What is true about the mammoth's body?

a. It was damaged while it was at the store.
b. It was taken to the store by helicopter.
c. Yuri sold it to the store owner.

∧ Some think mammoths died out because the Earth became too warm. Others think humans hunted them to extinction.

REFERENCE 3. The word *They* in paragraph C refers to _____.

a. mammoths
b. scientists
c. Yuri and his sons

INFERENCE 4. Which of the following can be inferred from the passage?

a. Lyuba died at the same time as her mother.
b. The mammoth died when the Ice Age ended.
c. Yuri's wife's name was Lyuba.

DETAIL 5. How did Lyuba die?

a. She was attacked by another animal.
b. Hunters killed her.
c. She died when she fell.

SEQUENCING B. Number the events (a–f) in the order they happened (1–6).

a. _____ Dogs ate part of the mammoth.

b. _____ Scientists began to study the mammoth.

c. _____ The mammoth's body was taken to a museum.

d. _____ Yuri's cousin sold the mammoth.

e. _____ The police arrived to take the mammoth away.

f. _____ Yuri's sons found a mammoth's body.

Understanding Passive Sentences

Reading passages often include a mix of active and passive sentences. In active sentences, *the subject* is the "**doer**" of the action. In passive sentences, *the subject* is the **receiver** of the action. The doer, if it is stated at all, usually follows **by**. Look at these examples and notice how passive sentences are formed.

Active	**Passive**
The boys <u>found</u> a mammoth.	*A mammoth* <u>was found</u> (by the boys).
The man's cousin <u>had sold</u> it.	*It* <u>had been sold</u> (by the man's cousin).
Scientists <u>will study</u> it.	*It* <u>will be studied</u> (by scientists).

UNDERSTANDING PASSIVE

A. Read the sentences below. Circle the "doer" of each action.

1. In the 19th century, some people found over 250 paintings in a cave in Rouffignac, France.
2. These incredible pictures were painted by early humans.
3. Scientists have dated the artwork to 11,000 B.C.
4. Almost 160 of the paintings show early man with mammoths.
5. The caves have been visited by tourists since the 1950s.
6. In 1979, the cave site was made a World Heritage Site by UNESCO.

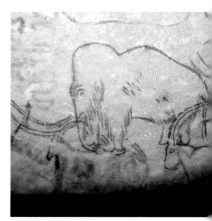

⌃ **A painting of a mammoth in the Rouffignac cave**

UNDERSTANDING PASSIVE

B. Choose the correct words to complete the sentences. Then check your answers in Reading A.

1. Dogs *had eaten / had been eaten* part of the tail.
2. The body *took / was taken* by helicopter to a museum.
3. The mammoth *sent / was sent* to the Netherlands and Japan.
4. Further studies *will explain / will be explained* how mammoths like Lyuba lived.

CRITICAL THINKING Discussing Pros and Cons

▶ Work with a partner. Some scientists want to bring extinct animals, like mammoths, back to life. List arguments for and against this.

Arguments for	Arguments against

▶ Discuss with another pair. Do you think extinct animals should be brought back to life? Why or why not?

COMPLETION **A.** Complete the information. Circle the correct words.

Close your eyes. Can you ¹**disappear** / **imagine** a crocodile so big that it eats dinosaurs? Scientists say such a crocodile really did live 110 million years ago, but it ²**disappeared** / **imagined** from Earth even before the dinosaurs became extinct. They call it "SuperCroc."

In 2000, a team of researchers found some SuperCroc bones in the Sahara Desert. After some ³**perfect** / **further** searching, they had enough bones to make up 50 percent of SuperCroc's skeleton.

∧ **A "SuperCroc" skeleton at a museum in Paris, France**

The scientists studied the bones ⁴**owner** / **in detail**. They learned that SuperCroc grew to about 8,000 kilograms and that its strong jaws and teeth were ⁵**nearby** / **perfect** for catching prey. The bones are now in museums, so people can learn about this amazing animal.

COMPLETION **B.** Complete the sentences. Choose the correct words.

1. If something is **nearby**, it is _____ you.
   a. close to   b. far from

2. You would probably go to a **store** to _____.
   a. see a sick friend   b. buy something

3. The **owner** of a restaurant _____.
   a. has already bought it   b. plans to buy it

4. If something is **perfect**, you probably want to _____.
   a. change it   b. keep it that way

COLLOCATIONS **C.** There are many phrases that begin with *in*, e.g., **in detail**. Complete the sentences using the words in the box.

action	danger	detail	fact

1. If you zoom in on this image, you can see it in _____.
2. There are many animals today that are in _____ of becoming extinct.
3. We went to the stadium to see the players in _____.
4. *Tylosaurus* was huge. In _____, it was bigger than most dinosaurs.

BEFORE YOU READ

LABELING **A.** Read the information below. Then label the picture with the numbers in **bold**. Write **1–5** in the circles.

At 14 meters long, *Tylosaurus* was one of the biggest sea monsters ever. Scientists know that it had great **(1) jaws** and big **(2) teeth**. Studies of its **(3) stomach** contents show it ate fish, birds, and even sharks. It used its long **(4) tail** to push itself through the water, and its two shorter **(5) fins** to change direction. *Tylosaurus* was not related to the dinosaurs, but it lived and became extinct around the same time.

PREDICTING **B.** Look quickly at the headings, pictures, and captions of the reading passage. Answer the questions below. Then read the passage to check your answers.

1 How many "monsters of the deep" does the passage mention?

2. What do you think was unusual about each creature?

∧ A *Tylosaurus* reaches for a shark with its great jaws.

MONSTERS
OF THE DEEP

A *Sea monsters are not just imaginary. Millions of years ago, real monsters actually lived on Earth.*

Eyes in the Dark

B *Temnodontosaurus* was **definitely** an unusual animal. Its name means "cutting-tooth lizard," and with good reason—it had very big teeth. It also had some of the largest eyes in nature. They were over 25 centimeters across! With such big eyes, *Temnodontosaurus* could easily find its food in the dark water.

Terror of the Deep

C *Kronosaurus*—the "Kronos lizard"—lived in the seas that once **covered** Australia. But it probably used its fins to **climb** out of the water and lay its eggs on land. Its head was two meters long, and its teeth were as big as bananas! The main purpose of strong jaws and teeth like these was to catch smaller animals. In fact, *Kronosaurus* was one of the most dangerous predators[1] of all time.

The Stalker[2]

D Known as the "lord of the seas," *Thalassomedon* was a large sea monster with a very long neck. It also had a special **way** of **hunting** fish: It carried stones in its stomach! These helped keep the largest part of its body and tail down in the dark water. **Meanwhile**, its long neck slowly **rose** up **toward** the fish. The fish didn't have a chance to get away from *Thalassomedon*. They couldn't see the sea monster until it was too late!

---

1 A **predator** is an animal that hunts and eats other animals.
2 To **stalk** someone or something is to follow slowly and quietly.

Kronosaurus

Thalassomedon

Temnodontosaurus

A. Choose the best answer for each question.

INFERENCE

1. What can we infer about *Temnodontosaurus*?

a. Its teeth were very sharp.
b. It only ate plants.
c. It was bigger than *Kronosaurus*.

INFERENCE

2. Around how long were the teeth of *Kronosaurus*?

a. two meters
b. 20 centimeters
c. 5 centimeters

REFERENCE

3. In paragraph D, the word *These* refers to _____.

a. fish
b. stones
c. ways to catch fish

DETAIL

4. What is unusual about *Thalassomedon*?

a. It laid its eggs on land.
b. It had very large eyes.
c. It had a very long neck.

> *Kronosaurus* was the largest sea reptile that ever lived.

DETAIL

5. Why did the fish not have a chance to get away from *Thalassomedon*?

a. The fish were not as fast as *Thalassomedon*.
b. *Thalassomedon* attacked the fish from above.
c. The fish didn't see *Thalassomedon* as it came near.

EVALUATING STATEMENTS

B. Are the following statements true or false, or is the information not given in the reading? Circle **T** (true), **F** (false), or **NG** (not given).

1. *Temnodontosaurus* got its name from its large eyes.   T F NG

2. *Temnodontosaurus* could see well in dark water.   T F NG

3. *Kronosaurus* spent all of its life in the water.   T F NG

4. *Kronosaurus* became extinct before *Thalassomedon*.   T F NG

5. *Thalassomedon* used stones to help it hunt.   T F NG

6. The three sea monsters sometimes attacked each other.   T F NG

READING SKILL

Organizing Information (2)—A Chart

Much like a concept map (see Unit 7), a chart helps you organize information in a visual way. It can be useful to take notes on the key details of a passage in a chart because it is a good way to "see" and remember the information you want to compare or contrast.

ANALYZING **A.** Look back at Reading B. What information is important to remember? Underline the key details about each sea creature.

ORGANIZING INFORMATION **B.** Complete the chart using information from Reading B. Write one word in each space.

	Temnodontosaurus	Kronosaurus	Thalassomedon
Meaning of name	"cutting-1_____ lizard"	"Kronos 5_____"	"lord of the 9_____"
Unusual characteristics	had very large 2_____ and 3_____	had teeth the size of 6_____	had a very long 10_____ and 11_____ in its stomach
Special abilities	could easily see its 4_____ in the dark water	could 7_____ smaller animals with its strong 8_____	was able to get close to 12_____ without being seen

CRITICAL THINKING Ranking

▶ If they lived today, how dangerous would these sea monsters be to humans? Rank them from 1 (most dangerous) to 3 (least dangerous).

_____ Temnodontosaurus

_____ Kronosaurus

_____ Thalassomedon

▶ Discuss with a partner and explain your reasons.

∧ **Thalassomedon** surprises a school of fish.

COMPLETION **A.** Complete the information using the correct form of the words in the box. One word is extra.

| cover | definitely | hunt | rise | toward | way |

For hundreds of years, people have heard reports of monsters that
¹_____ out of the sea to attack ships. Many people now think these "monsters" were probably giant squid.

Giant squid are ²_____ one of the most unusual creatures found in the ocean. They can grow up to 13 meters in length. They also have the largest eyes of any animal in the world. This helps them ³_____ for deep-sea

△ **A researcher swims with a giant squid.**

fish. When it is attacked, the giant squid has a very clever ⁴_____ of escaping. It shoots dark ink ⁵_____ its attacker. This makes it difficult for the predator to see, and gives the squid the chance to get away.

DEFINITIONS **B.** Match each word with its definition.

1. **climb** •   • a. (adv) at the same time
2. **cover** •   • b. (v) to move to a higher place
3. **meanwhile** •   • c. (v) to be on top of something

WORD PARTS **C.** The suffix *-ward* indicates direction, e.g., **toward**. Complete the sentences using the words in the box. One word is extra.

| backward | downward | forward | upward |

1. I'm really looking _____ to the weekend. I need a rest.
2. Though they can hop at great speed, kangaroos are unable to walk _____.
3. Hot-air balloons move _____ as the air inside the balloon gets hotter.

⌄ A three-meter-long ichthyosaur fossil on display at a museum in Germany

ICHTHYOSAURS

BEFORE YOU WATCH

PREVIEWING **A.** Read the information. The words and phrases in **bold** appear in the video. Match each word with its definition.

Ichthyosaurs were huge prehistoric creatures that lived in the sea. The first ichthyosaurs looked a lot like lizards, but later they **developed** fish-like tails. Ichthyosaurs had **skulls** that were long and **narrow**. Their teeth were very sharp, and they had huge eyes. One type of ichthyosaur, *Temnodontosaurus*, had larger eyes than any other known animal.

1. develop •   • a. (adj) the opposite of *wide*

2. narrow •   • b. (v) to grow or change over time

3. skull •   • c. (n) the bones in the head

PREDICTING **B.** Work with a partner. Guess answers to the questions below. Note your ideas.

1. What do you think ichthyosaurs ate? _____

2. Why do you think they had such big eyes? _____

3. How fast do you think they could swim? _____

GIST **A.** Watch the video. Check your guesses in Before You Watch B.

COMPLETION **B.** Watch the video again. Complete the notes about ichthyosaurs using information from the video.

Ichthyosaurs

- first appeared ^{1}_____ million years ago
- name means "^{2}_____-lizard"
- smallest were only ^{3}_____ long; biggest ^{4}_____ long
- large tail helped them swim fast
- became extinct ^{5}_____ million years before dinosaurs died out

< ***Opthalmosaurus*** was a six-meter-long ichthyosaur.

CRITICAL THINKING Applying Ideas   In countries around the world, there are stories of huge prehistoric creatures that still exist today. Can you think of any examples? Do you think any of these stories could be true? Note your ideas below. Then discuss with a partner.

_____

_____

VOCABULARY REVIEW

Do you remember the meanings of these words? Check (✓) the ones you know. Look back at the unit and review any words you're not sure of.

Reading A

☐ disappear   ☐ further   ☐ imagine   ☐ in detail

☐ nearby   ☐ owner   ☐ perfect   ☐ store

Reading B

☐ climb   ☐ cover   ☐ definitely*   ☐ hunt

☐ meanwhile   ☐ rise   ☐ toward   ☐ way

*Academic Word List

12

TECHNOLOGY

Many robots today, such as the sticky-bot, are designed to copy the movements of animals.

WARM UP

Discuss these questions with a partner.

1. What kinds of technology do you often use?

2. What kinds of things do you think people will do differently a hundred years from now?

BEFORE YOU READ

DISCUSSION **A.** What can robots do that humans can't? What can humans do that robots can't? Use the words and phrases from the box, and add your own ideas.

climb stairs	**feel emotions**	**talk to people**
jump	**play soccer**	**run**
take care of people	**drive cars**	**dance**
walk up walls	**learn new things**	**write poems**

SCANNING **B.** Look quickly at the reading. Which of the things above are mentioned? Do you think today's robots can do them? Read the passage to check your ideas.

❮ The robot ASIMO can move in a similar way to a human.

THE ROBOTS ARE COMING!

A   You have probably seen robots in movies such as *Star Wars* or *Transformers*. But soon, robots may be part of our **daily** lives. Today's scientists are working on robots with various skills. For example, it is likely that robots will soon help take care of children or the elderly,[1] or do dangerous jobs such as fighting fires.

B   Early robots were made to do **simple** things, mainly in **factories**. Since then, robots have changed a lot. Humans **operated** these early robots. Today's robots—like Honda's ASIMO—work on their own. ASIMO can run, climb stairs, and dance. Boston Dynamics' Atlas robot can run fast, jump, and even do backflips[2]—all on two legs!

C   Then there are robots designed to be like humans. These robots have faces and can also talk. Such robots can learn new things, and show us how they "feel." Sophia—a social robot—has a face that looks so human she sometimes makes people feel **uncomfortable**.

---

1   Someone who is **elderly** is old.
2   A **backflip** is a movement that involves jumping, spinning around in the air, and landing again on your feet.

Boston Dynamics' Atlas robot is the same height and weight as an average human.

> Social robots like Sophia can show emotions.

Animal-bots

D Scientists aren't just building humanlike robots. They are also making robots that look and **act** like animals.

E At NASA, for example, scientists have made a robot snake. These snake-bots can enter holes and move over **rough** ground. They might one day help scientists look for **signs** of life on Mars. Other animal robots include the frog-bot, which can jump over objects, and the sticky-bot, which can walk up walls. There are also doglike robots, like SpotMini, which have four legs and can run at high speed. Who knows? Perhaps in the future, we'll all have our own robot pet.

> **SpotMini can walk and run just like a real dog.**

A. Choose the best answer for each question.

GIST

1. The passage is mainly about _____.

   a. things robots can do

   b. famous robots from movies

   c. how to make your own robot

PURPOSE

2. What is the purpose of paragraph B?

   a. to describe how the first robots worked

   b. to explain how today's robots are different from early robots

   c. to give an example of a robot that worked in a factory

REFERENCE

3. In paragraph C, the word *they* refers to _____.

   a. humans

   b. robots

   c. scientists

△ **Snake-bots can climb over objects that block their path.**

DETAIL

4. Which of the following robots would best be able to move over a large rock in its path?

   a. frog-bot

   b. Sophia

   c. SpotMini

DETAIL

5. Why was the snake-bot created?

   a. to help scientists learn more about real snakes

   b. as a toy for young children

   c. to help study other planets

SCANNING

B. Scan the reading for each of the robots in the box (a–f). Complete the sentences using the correct options.

a. ASIMO	b. Atlas	c. Snake-bot
d. Sophia	e. SpotMini	f. Sticky-bot

1. _____ is a social robot that can talk and show emotions.

2. _____ can climb walls.

3. _____ and _____ can run on two legs.

4. _____ was developed by NASA.

5. _____ looks and moves like a dog.

Identifying Examples

Writers often use examples to support their ideas or help explain difficult concepts. Finding examples in a text will help you understand the writer's main ideas. Words that show where examples are in a text include *for example, like,* and *such as.*

IDENTIFYING EXAMPLES   **A.**   Look back at Reading A. Find and circle all of the words and phrases that introduce examples.

IDENTIFYING EXAMPLES   **B.**   Find and write the example(s) of each thing below given in the reading passage.

1. two movies with robots (paragraph A) _____, _____

2. two jobs that future robots might do (paragraph A) _____, _____

3. a robot that works on its own (paragraph B) _____

4. a robot created by NASA that acts like an animal (paragraph E) _____

5. a doglike robot (paragraph E) _____

IDENTIFYING EXAMPLES   **C.**   Complete the information using examples from the box.

> a. he could be seen at the Henry Ford Museum
> b. "I am Elektro" and "My brain is bigger than yours."
> c. sitting, barking, and begging for food
> d. he could walk, talk, and move his arms and legs

One of the first humanlike robots was Elektro. He was built between 1937 and 1939 and could do many simple human actions. For example, [1]_____. He was first seen at the New York World's Fair in 1939. He was joined by Sparko, a robot dog that could do tricks, such as [2]_____. In 1992, a dance band made a song that used some things Elektro said, like, [3]_____. Elektro's home is at the Mansfield Memorial Museum in Ohio, United States. However, he often travels to other museums. For instance, in 2013, [4]_____.

CRITICAL THINKING Justifying Opinions

▶ List three jobs you think robots will someday do instead of humans.

_____   _____   _____

▶ Compare your jobs with a partner. Give reasons for your choices.

COMPLETION **A.** Complete the information using the words in the box.

act	rough	signs	simple	uncomfortable

For humans, walking is usually a very ¹_____ task.
But for robots, it's very difficult—especially over
²_____ ground. Researchers are working to help
robots walk better by giving them machine parts that
³_____ like human bones and muscles.

Walking on four legs is much simpler. Robot pets
have already been developed and are becoming
more and more popular. They move, cry, sense
your movements, and can even learn basic
words. But there are no ⁴_____ yet that
robot pets will replace real ones. Many people
find that robot pets make them feel ⁵_____.

∧ **Aibo is a puppy-sized pet robot
dog developed by Sony.**

DEFINITIONS **B.** Complete the sentences. Choose the correct options.

1. An example of a **daily** event is _____.
   a. eating dinner   b. going on vacation

2. A **factory** is a place where things are _____.
   a. made   b. sold

3. If you **operate** a machine, you _____ it.
   a. fix   b. use

COLLOCATIONS **C.** The nouns in the box are often used with the adjective **daily**. Complete the
sentences using the correct words.

events	exercise	work

1. A big part of my daily _____ involves using a computer.
2. To stay fit and healthy, it's important to do daily _____.
3. Rather than newspapers, many people use social media to keep up to date with
   daily _____ around the world.

BEFORE YOU READ

DISCUSSION **A.** Read the title of the reading passage. In what ways do you think life will be different in 2045? Discuss with a partner and list your ideas.

SKIMMING **B.** Skim the reading. Which of your ideas in activity A are mentioned? What other things does the reading passage discuss?

⌃ **By 2045, many homes could have a "smart" kitchen.**

HOW WILL WE LIVE IN 2045?

A   Welcome to life in the future! You get up in the morning and look into the **mirror**. You've **recently** had a new anti-aging treatment, so you look like a 30-year-old. And many people your age could live to be 120 now, so—at 60—you're not old at all.

B   Science has also found amazing ways to keep people healthy. Nanotechnology[1] can help cure many illnesses, including cancer. And if any part of your body is unhealthy, you can "grow" a new one in a laboratory.

C   As you **get dressed**, you say to your shirt, "**Turn** red." It becomes red. In 2045, "smart" clothes contain nanoparticles that carry **electricity**. So you can **program** clothes to change colors or patterns.

D   On the way to the kitchen, you want to call a friend. Your cell phone is by the window because it gets its energy from the sun. But you don't need to **pick up** the phone. You can just touch your jacket sleeve[2] to make the call.

E   It's breakfast time. You reach for the milk, but a **voice** says, "Don't drink that!" Your fridge knows the milk is old, and tells the supermarket to replace it. Ten minutes later, it's delivered by a drone.[3]

F   As you leave for work, the lights turn off by themselves. Your home goes into "sleep" mode to save energy. In 2045, cars drive themselves, so you just tell your driverless car where you want to go.

G   Will all this come true? Perhaps the future is much closer than we think.

---

1   **Nanotechnology** is the science of very small things that are measured in nanometers (one billionth of a meter).
2   The **sleeves** of a shirt or jacket are the parts that cover your arms.
3   A **drone** is a kind of flying robot.

> Companies like Volkswagen are already designing self-driving cars.

A. Choose the best answer for each question.

DETAIL
1. What does the writer say about aging in the future?

   a. Age 60 will not be thought of as old.
   b. People who are 120 will be very healthy.
   c. People who are 60 can expect to live 120 more years.

DETAIL
2. What is NOT mentioned as a reason people are healthier in 2045?

   a. Serious illnesses have been cured.
   b. Robot doctors work in hospitals.
   c. New body parts can be grown by scientists.

REFERENCE
3. In paragraph C, *It* refers to _____.

   a. electricity
   b. your shirt
   c. the pattern

In the future, many deliveries will be carried out by drones.

DETAIL
4. Which of the following predictions is NOT mentioned in the passage?

   a. Homes will use less energy.
   b. Clothes will be able to change their patterns.
   c. People won't use cars.

INFERENCE
5. In paragraph E, what says, "Don't drink that!"?

   a. the milk
   b. the fridge
   c. the drone

SHORT ANSWERS
B. Write short answers for these questions. Use information from the reading passage.

1. In 2045, what has helped cure cancer?

_____

2. Where does the cell phone get energy from?

_____

3. After the fridge orders milk, how long does it take to be delivered?

_____

4. What is special about cars in the future?

_____

Understanding Prefixes

A prefix is one or more letters (e.g., *un-*, *mis-*, *dis-*, *inter-*, *trans-*) that can be added to the beginning of a word to make a new word (e.g., *e-* + *book* = *e-book*, and *pre-* + *program* = *preprogram*). Understanding prefixes can help you guess the meaning of unfamiliar words and build your vocabulary. Some words with prefixes require a hyphen (e.g., *self-taught*, *ex-president*), so it's best to check in a dictionary.

UNDERSTANDING PREFIXES

A. Look at the prefixes, meanings, and examples. Write a new word for each prefix using words in the box. Check your words in a dictionary.

social	view	~~kind~~	star

	Prefix	Meanings	Examples	Your ideas:
1.	un-	not	uncomfortable	unkind
2.	re-	again	reprogram	
3.	super-	above	supercomputer	
4.	anti-	against	anti-virus	

DEFINITIONS

B. Find words in Reading B that contain these prefixes. Write the full word and then a definition.

1. anti- (paragraph A) Word: _____
   Definition: _____

2. un- (paragraph B)   Word: _____
   Definition: _____

3. re- (paragraph E)   Word: _____
   Definition: _____

4. super (paragraph E) Word: _____
   Definition: _____

CRITICAL THINKING Rating Predictions   Look back at Reading B. Rate each prediction about 2045 below 1–3 (1 = very likely, 3 = very unlikely). Compare your answers with a partner, and discuss your reasons.

_____ many people live to be 120   _____ you can grow new body parts in a lab

_____ clothes can change colors   _____ cell phones get energy from the sun

_____ every home has a smart fridge   _____ most cars are driverless

DEFINITIONS   **A.** Complete the definitions using the correct form of the words in the box.

electricity	get dressed	mirror	pick up
program	recently	turn	voice

1. If you look into a(n) _____, you see yourself.

2. You hear a person's _____ when they speak.

3. When you _____ something, you lift it up.

4. When you _____, you put on your clothes.

5. If something _____ red, it becomes red.

6. You _____ a machine by giving it instructions so it performs an action.

7. If something happened _____, it happened not very long ago.

8. _____ is energy that travels through wires and is used to operate machines.

COMPLETION   **B.** Complete the information using the correct form of the words in activity A.

When you ¹_____ in the morning, you may soon choose your clothes based on what they can do rather than how they look. "Smart clothes" of the future will ²_____ energy from the sun into ³_____. This power could be used to charge your phone or computer. Some clothes could even be ⁴_____ to heat up or to change color.

∧ **Current smart clothes are able to monitor the wearer's heart rate.**

WORD USAGE   **C.** The phrasal verb **pick up** has more than one meaning. Look at the definitions (1–3) below. Match each one with an example sentence (a–c).

1. pick up (v) to collect someone from a place, usually in a car   •

2. pick up (v) to learn naturally   •

3. pick up (v) to lift something   •

• a. The robot is able to pick up objects from the floor.

• b. I picked up Spanish pretty quickly when I lived in Madrid.

• c. I'll pick you up from school at 4 p.m.

A SOCIAL ROBOT

‹ Sophia is one of the world's most advanced social robots.

BEFORE YOU WATCH

PREVIEWING **A.** Read the information. The words in **bold** appear in the video. Match each word with its definition.

A social robot is a robot that can communicate with a human. Many can create humanlike **facial expressions** that show their **emotions**. Some social robots can also "read" human faces. For example, they can tell if we are sad and can say something to make us happy. A robot named Sophia is one of the most **advanced** social robots. Many believe that robots like her could become common in homes of the future.

1. advanced   •   • a. our feelings, e.g., anger, sadness
2. facial expression •   • b. modern; with the latest technology
3. emotions   •   • c. a way people show their feelings, e.g., smiling

DISCUSSION **B.** What do you think social robots like Sophia could be used for in the future? Work with a partner and note some ideas below.

_____

_____

_____

WHILE YOU WATCH

GIST **A.** Watch the video. Which of your ideas in Before You Watch B are mentioned? Note any other uses for social robots below.

SHORT ANSWER **B.** Watch the video again. Note answers to the questions.

   1. What happened to Sophia in February 2016?

   2. What does Sophia's name mean?

   3. How many different facial expressions can Sophia make?

   4. What happened to Sophia in 2018?

CRITICAL THINKING Evaluating Ideas What are the advantages of having more robots in our daily lives? What are the disadvantages? Note some ideas in the chart below. Then discuss with a partner.

Advantages of Robots	Disadvantages of Robots

VOCABULARY REVIEW

Do you remember the meanings of these words? Check (✓) the ones you know. Look back at the unit and review any words you're not sure of.

Reading A

☐ act ☐ daily ☐ factory ☐ operate
☐ rough ☐ sign ☐ simple ☐ uncomfortable

Reading B

☐ electricity ☐ get dressed ☐ mirror ☐ pick up
☐ program ☐ recently ☐ turn ☐ voice

Photo and Illustration Credits

Cover teamLab Borderless, **3** teamLab Borderless, **4–5** Frans Lanting/NGIC, **7** Erik Harrison/NGIC, **8** ESO/M. Kornmesser, **9** Bryan Bedder/Getty Images Entertainment/Getty Images, **10** Tristan3D/Shutterstock.com, Amanda Carden/Shutterstock.com, **11** ESO/M. Kornmesser, **12** Babak Tafreshi/NGIC, **13** Robert Harding Picture Library Ltd/Alamy Stock Photo, **14–15** MondoWorks, **16** DEA/G. Dagli Orti/De Agostini/Getty Images, **17** Takaji Ochi/VWPICS/Visual&Written SL/Alamy Stock Photo, **18** Tsado/Alamy Stock Photo, **19** NASA/JPL-Caltech/SETI Institute, **20** NASA, **21** Mario Laporta/AFP/Getty Images, **22–23** Michael Brochstein/SOPA Images/Getty Images, **24** Gilbert Carrasquillo/Getty Images Entertainment/Getty Images, **25** Bobby Bank/Wire Image/Getty Images, **27** Mitchell Leff/Getty Images Sports/Getty Images, **28** (tl) Manexcatalapiedra/Moment/Getty Images, **28** (tr) Julian Eales/Alamy Stock Photo, **28** (cl) Maxim Tatarinov/Alamy Stock Photo, **28** (cr) Andrew Wood/Alamy Stock Photo, **28** (bl) Helen Sessions/Alamy Stock Photo, **28** (br) Etienne Voss/Alamy Stock Photo, **29** Strdel/AFP/Getty Images, **30** Svetlana Foote/Alamy Stock Photo, **31** StockFood GmbH/Alamy Stock Photo, **32** Keith Dannemiller/Alamy Stock Photo, **33** Christopher Furlong/Getty Images News/Getty Images, **35** Jim Richardson/NGIC, **36–37** Nora Shawki/NGIC, **38** Dallet-Alba/Alamy Stock Photo, **40** Joseph Sohm/Corbis NX/Getty Images, **41** Joel Sartore/NGIC, **42** Doug Gimesy/NGIC, **44** Viviane Moos/Corbis News/Getty Images, **46** Joel Sartore/NGIC, **46** Joel Sartore/NGIC, **47** AP Images/Carsten Rehder/picture–alliance/dpa, **49** Ryan Rossotto/StockTrek Images/NGIC, **50–51** Raymond Wong/NGIC, **52** (t) Priit Vesilind/NGIC, **52** (b) Emory Kritstof/NGIC, **53** World History Archive/Alamy Stock Photo, **55** Topical Press Agency/Stringer/Hulton Archive/Getty Images, **56–57** Allstar Picture Library/Alamy Stock Photo, **57** Mark Thiessen/NGIC, **58** AF Archive/Alamy Stock Photo, **59** Underwood Archives/Archive Photos/Getty Images, **61** Brett Seymour, EUA/ARGO NGO, **62** NGIC, **63** Max Aguilera–Hellweg/NGIC, **64** Cultura RM Exclusive/Sigrid Gombert/Cultura Exclusive/Getty Images Plus/Getty Images, **65** Joshua Roberts/Bloomberg/Getty Images, **67** Tobkatrina/Shutterstock.com, **68–69** Monty Rakusen/Cultura/Getty Images, **70** Pablo Paul/Alamy Stock Photo, **71** Ton Koene/Alamy Stock Photo, **72** Florea Paul/Alamy Stock Photo, **73** nobeastsofierce/Shutterstock.com, **75** Diane Cook and Len Jenshel/NGIC, **76** Benno Kraehahn, **77** Sascha Steinbach/Getty Images Entertainment/Getty Images, **78** Markus Schwerer/Plant-for-the-Planet, **79** Plant-for-the-Planet, **80** DPA picture alliance/Alamy Stock Photo, **81** Marco Uliana/Alamy Stock Photo, **82** Helene Schmitz/NGIC, **83** (all) Helene Schmitz/NGIC, **84** Frans Lanting/NGIC, **85** Paul Starosta/Corbis Documentary/Getty Images, **86** Richard Nowitz/NGIC, **87** Frans Lanting/NGIC, **88** Stock Illustrations.com/Alamy Stock Photo, **89** Andrew Toth/Getty Images Entertainment/Getty Images, **90** Magnus Wennman/NGIC, **91** Michael Nichols/NGIC, **92** Joel Sartore/NGIC, **94** PeopleImages/iStock/Getty Images, **95** Mike Theiss/NGIC, **96** Chris the Composer/iStock/Getty Images, **97** (t) Chris Madden/Alamy Stock Photo, **97** (b) viphotos/Shutterstock.com, **98** Chris Madden/Alamy Stock Photo, **100** Chris Johns/NGIC, **101** PhotoAlto/Frederic Cirou/PhotoAlto Agency RF Collections/Getty Images, **103** Jason Edwards/NGIC, **104–105** Frans Lanting/NGIC, **106** Martin Ruegner/Photographer Choice/Getty Images, **107** Frans Lanting/NGIC, **108** Theo Allofs/Corbis Documentary/Getty Images, **109** Breck P. Kent/Animals Animals/Earth Scenes/NGIC, **110** (all) Joel Sartore, National Geographic Photo Ark/NGIC, **111** 101cats/E+/Getty Images, **112** Joel Sartore/NGIC, **113** John Warburton-Lee/AWL Images/Getty Images Plus/Getty Images, **114** Barcroft/Barcroft Media/Getty Images, **115** Paul Nicklen/NGIC, **117** Steve Raymer/NGIC, **118** Robert Harding Picture Library/NGIC, **119** Dinodia Photos/Alamy Stock Photo, **120** Philippe Lissac/Corbis Documentary/Getty Images, **121** robuart/Shutterstock.com, **122** daewoosao/Shutterstock.com, **123** Robert Harding/Alamy Stock Photo, **124** Fernando G. Baptista/NGIC, **125** Fernando G. Baptista/NGIC, **126** Atlantide Phototravel/Corbis Documentary/Getty Images, **128** Michael Dunning/Photographer's Choice/Getty Images, **129** Bob Berry/Alamy Stock Photo, **131** Susana Guzman/Alamy Stock Photo, **132–133** Trevor Mogg/Alamy Stock Photo, **134** Chip Somodevilla/Getty Images News/Getty Images, **135** Jhaz Photography/Shutterstock.com, **137** Rob Griffith/AFP/Getty Images, **138** Daniel J Bryant/Moment/Getty Images, **139** Nancy G Fire Photography, Nancy Greifenhagen/Alamy Stock Photo, **140** Roger Hill/Barcroft Media/Getty Images, **141** Ian Hitchcock/Getty Images News/Getty Images, **142** Vince Cavataio/Perspectives/Getty Images, **143** Jim Reed/NGIC, **145** Raul Martin/NGIC, **146** International Mammoth Committee/NGIC, **147** (b) Ryan Rossotto/NGIC, **147** (tr) Kazuhiko Sano/NGIC, **148** Science Picture Co/Collection Mix Subjects/Getty Images, **149** Print Collector/Hulton Archive/Getty Images, **150** Sergey Skleznev/Alamy Stock Photo, **151** Matte FX, Matte FX Inc./NGIC, **152–153** (all) Matte FX, Matte FX Inc./NGIC, **154** Sergey Krasovskiy/Stocktrek Images/Getty Images, **155** Matte FX, Matte FX Inc./NGIC, **156** Brian J. Skerry/NGIC, **157** Holger Hollemann/picture alliance/Getty Images, **158** Stocktrek Images/NGIC, **159** Robert Clark/NGIC, **160** Wenn Rights Ltd/Alamy Stock Photo, **161** (t) Kiyoshi Ota/Bloomberg/Getty Images, **161** (b) STR/NurPhoto/Getty Images, **162** Laura Chiesa/Pacific Press/Getty Images, **163** NASA, **164** Sherman Oaks Antique Mall/Archive Photos/Getty Images, **165** Kazuhiro Nogi/AFP/Getty Images, **166** Tetra Images, LLC/Alamy Stock Photo, **167** Uli Deck/picture alliance/Getty Images, **168** Slavoljub Pantelic/Shutterstock.com, **170** Kiyoshi Ota/Bloomberg/Getty Images, **171** Isaac Lawrence/AFP/Getty Images, **172** ITAR TASS News Agency/Alamy Stock Photo

NGIC – National Geographic Image Collection

Text Credits

9 Based on information from "Rock from Another Star System Is Unlike Anything Seen Before," by Michael Greshko: news.nationalgeographic.com, **15** Adapted from "Unsolved Mystery: Atlantis," by Michael N. Smith and Debora L. Smith: NGK, March 2005, and based on information from "Does New Theory Pinpoint Lost City of Atlantis?" by Simon Worrall: news.nationalgeographic.com, **23** Adapted from "Nathan's Famous Hot Dog Eating Contest," by Ryan Schleeter: news.nationalgeographic.com, **29** Based on information from "Hot Pod," by Catherine L. Barker: NGM, May 2007, **37** Based on information provided by Nora Shawki, **43** Adapted from interviews from joelsartore.com, **51** Adapted from "Why Is the Titanic Vanishing?" by Robert D. Ballard: NGM, December 2004, **57** Based on information provided by Corey Jaskolski, **64** Adapted from "Disease Detective," by Marylou Tousignant: NGE, March 2010, **69** Adapted from "On the Case," by Dana Jensen and Natasha Metzler: NGE, October 2008, **77** Based on information from "Teenager Is on Track to Plant a Trillion Trees," by Laura Parker: news.nationalgeographic.com, **82** Adapted from "Fatal Attraction," by Carl Zimmer: NGM, March 2010, **91** Adapted from "How to Decode Your Dreams," by Sarah Wassner: NGK, August 2005, **97** Adapted from "Optical Illusions," NGE, April 2005, **105** Based on information from "Destination Antarctica: Emperor Penguins," by Crispin Boyer: NGK, April 2009, **111** Adapted from "What's So Funny?" by Aline Alexander Newman: NGK, April 2006, **119** Based on information from "Taj Mahal," nationalgeographic.com, **124** Based on information from "Brunelleschi's Dome," by Tom Mueller: NGM, February 2014, **133** Adapted from "Weather Gone Wild," by Peter Miller: NGM, September 2012, **139** Adapted from "Ten Freaky Forces of Nature," by Douglas E. Richards: NGK, September 2008, **147** Adapted from "Mystery of the Frozen Mammoth," by Kristin Baird Rattini: NGK, May 2009, and "Ice Baby," by Tom Mueller: NGM, May 2009, **152** Based on information from "When Monsters Ruled the Deep," by Virginia Morell: NGM, December 2005, **161** Based on information from "Robot Revolution," by Douglas Richards: NGK, February 2008, and "Robots," by Chris Carroll: NGM, August 2011, **167** Based on information from "It's 2035," by Ruth Musgrave, NGK, September 2005

NGM = National Geographic Magazine, NGK = National Geographic Kids Magazine, NGE = National Geographic Explorer Magazine

Acknowledgments

The Authors and Publisher would like to thank the following teaching professionals for their valuable feedback during the development of the series.

Akiko Hagiwara, Tokyo University of Pharmacy and Life Sciences; **Albert Lehner**, University of Fukui; **Alexander Cameron**, Kyushu Sangyo University; **Amira Traish**, University of Sharjah; **Andrés López**, Colégio José Max León; **Andrew Gallacher**, Kyushu Sangyo University; **Angelica Hernandez**, Liceo San Agustin; **Angus Painter**, Fukuoka University; **Anouchka Rachelson**, Miami Dade College; **Ari Hayakawa**, Aoyama Gakuin University; **Atsuko Otsuki**, Senshu University; **Ayako Hisatsune**, Kanazawa Institute of Technology; **Bogdan Pavliy**, Toyama University of International Studies; **Braden Chase**, The Braden Chase Company; **Brian J. Damm**, Kanda Institute of Foreign Languages; **Carol Friend**, Mercer County Community College; **Catherine Yu**, CNC Language School; **Chad Godfrey**, Saitama Medical University; **Cheng-hao Weng**, SMIC Private School; **Chisako Nakamura**, Ryukoku University; **Chiyo Myojin**, Kochi University of Technology; **Chris Valvona**, Okinawa Christian College; **Claire DeFord**, Olympic College; **Davi Sukses**, Sutomo 1; **David Farnell**, Fukuoka University; **David Johnson**, Kyushu Sangyo University; **Debbie Sou**, Kwong Tai Middle School; **Devin Ferreira**, University of Central Florida; **Eden Kaiser**, Framingham State University; **Ellie Park**, CNC Language School; **Elvis Bartra García**, Corporación Educativa Continental; **Emiko Yamada**, Westgate Corporation; **Eri Tamura**, Ishikawa Prefectural University; **Fadwa Sleiman**, University of Sharjah; **Frank Gutsche**, Tohoku University; **Frank Lin**, Guangzhou Tufu Culture; **Gavin Young**, Iwate University; **Gerry Landers**, GA Tech Language Institute; **Ghada Ahmed**, University of Bahrain; **Grace Choi**, Grace English School; **Greg Bevan**, Fukuoka University; **Gregg McNabb**, Shizuoka Institute of Science and Technology; **Helen Roland**, Miami Dade College; **Hiroshi Ohashi**, Kyushu University; **Hiroyo Yoshida**, Toyo University; **Hojin Song**, GloLink Education; **Jackie Bae**, Plato Language School; **Jade Wong**, Belilios Public School; **James McCarron**, Chiba University; **Jane Kirsch**, INTO George Mason University; **Jenay Seymore**, Hong Ik University; **John Appleby**, Kanda Institute of Foreign Languages; **John Nevara**, Kagoshima University; **Jonathan Bronson**, Approach International Student Center; **Joseph Zhou**, UUabc; **Josh Brunotte**, Aichi Prefectural University; **Junjun Zhou**, Menaul School; **Kaori Yamamoto**; **Katarina Zorkic**, Rosemead College; **Keiko Miyagawa**, Meiji University; **Kevin Tang**, Ritsumeikan Asia Pacific University; **Kieran Julian**, Kanda Institute of Foreign Languages; **Kim Kawashima**, Olympic College; **Kyle Kumataka**, Ritsumeikan Asia Pacific University; **Kyosuke Shimamura**, Kurume University; **Lance Stilp**, Ritsumeikan Asia Pacific University; **Li Zhaoli**, Weifang No.7 Middle School; **Liza Armstrong**, University of Missouri; **Lucas Pignolet**, Ritsumeikan Asia Pacific University; **Luke Harrington**, Chiba University; **M. Lee**, KCC; **Maiko Berger**, Ritsumeikan Asia Pacific University; **Mandy Kan**, CNEC Christian College; **Mari Nakamura**, English Square; **Masako Kikukawa**, Doshisha University; **Matthew Fraser**, Westgate Corporation; **Mayuko Matsunuma**, Seijo University; **Michiko Imai**, Aichi University; **Mei-ho Chiu**, Soochow University; **Melissa Potts**, ELS Berkeley; **Monica Espinoza**, Torrance Adult School; **Ms. Manassara Riensumettharadol**, Kasetsart University; **My Uyen Tran**, Ho Chi Minh City University of Foreign Languages and Information Technology; **Narahiko Inoue**, Kyushu University; **Neil Witkin**, Kyushu Sangyo University; **Noriko Tomioka**, Kwansei University; **Olesya Shatunova**, Kanagawa University; **Patricia Fiene**, Midwestern Career College; **Patricia Nation**, Miami Dade College; **Patrick John Johnston**, Ritsumeikan Asia Pacific University; **Paula Snyder**, University of Missouri-Columbia; **Paul Hansen**, Hokkaido University; **Ping Zhang**, Beijing Royal School; **Reiko Kachi**, Aichi University / Chukyo University; **Robert Dykes**, Jin-ai University; **Rosanna Bird**, Approach International Student Center; **Ryo Takahira**, Kurume Fusetsu High School; **Samuel Taylor**, Kyushu Sangyo University; **Sandra Stein**, American University of Kuwait; **Sanooch Nathalang**, Thammasat University; **Sara Sulko**, University of Missouri; **Serena Lo**, Wong Shiu Chi Secondary School; **Shin Okada**, Osaka University; **Silvana Carlini**, Colégio Agostiniano Mendel; **Silvia Yafai**, ADVETI: Applied Tech High School; **Stella Millikan**, Fukuoka Women's University; **Summer Webb**, University of Colorado Boulder; **Susumu Hiramatsu**, Okayama University; **Suzanne Littlewood**, Zayed University; **Takako Kuwayama**, Kansai University; **Takashi Urabe**, Aoyama-Gakuin University; **Teo Kim**, OROMedu; **Tim Chambers**; **Toshiya Tanaka**, Kyushu University; **Trevor Holster**, Fukuoka University; **Wakako Takinami**, Tottori University; **Wayne Malcolm**, Fukui University of Technology; **Wendy Wish**, Valencia College; **Xiaoying Zhan**, Bejing Royal Foreign Language School; **Xingwu Chen**, Xueersi-TAL; **Yin Wang**, TAL Education Group; **Yohei Murayama**, Kagoshima University; **Yoko Sakurai**, Aichi University; **Yoko Sato**, Tokyo University of Agriculture and Technology; **Yoon-Ji Ahn**, Daks Education; **Yu-Lim Im**, Daks Education; **Yuriko Ueda**, Ryukoku University; **Yvonne Hodnett**, Australian College of Kuwait; **Yvonne Johnson**, UWCSEA Dover; **Zhang Lianzhong**, Beijing Foreign Studies University

GLOSSARY

These words are used in *Reading Explorer* to describe various reading and critical thinking skills.

Analyze	to study a text in detail, e.g., to identify key points, similarities, and differences
Apply	to think about how an idea might be useful in other ways, e.g., solutions to a problem
Classify	to arrange things in groups or categories, based on their characteristics
Evaluate	to examine different sides of an issue, e.g., reasons for and against something
Infer	to "read between the lines"—information the writer expresses indirectly
Interpret	to think about what a writer means by a certain phrase or expression
Justify	to give reasons for a personal opinion, belief, or decision
Rank	to put things in order based on criteria, e.g., size or importance
Reflect	to think deeply about what a writer is saying and how it compares with your own views
Relate	to consider how ideas in a text connect with your own personal experience
Scan	to look through a text to find particular words or information
Skim	to look at a text quickly to get an overall understanding of its main idea
Summarize	to give a brief statement of the main points of a text
Synthesize	to use information from more than one source to make a judgment or comparison

INDEX OF EXAM QUESTION TYPES

The activities in *Reading Explorer, Third Edition* provide comprehensive practice of several question types that feature in standardized tests such as TOEFL® and IELTS.

Common Question Types	IELTS	TOEFL®	Page(s)
Multiple choice (main idea, detail, reference, inference, vocabulary, paraphrasing)	✓	✓	11, 16, 25, 30, 38, 44, 53, 58, 65, 70, 78, 84, 92, 98, 107, 112, 117, 120, 126, 135, 140, 148, 154, 163, 168,
Completion (notes, diagram, chart)	✓		20, 48, 74, 79, 88, 93, 120, 121, 158
Completion (summary)	✓	✓	11, 53, 65, 98, 107, 144
Short answer	✓		16, 78, 116, 135, 168, 172
Matching headings / information	✓		25, 30, 34, 38, 58, 62, 92, 126, 140, 163
Categorizing (matching features)	✓	✓	102, 155
True / False / Not Given	✓		70, 112, 154
Rhetorical purpose		✓	25, 30, 38, 66, 78, 84, 98, 107, 112, 126, 135, 140, 163

The following tips will help you become a more successful reader.

1 Preview the text

Before you start reading a text, it's important to have some idea of the overall topic. Look at the title, photos, captions, and any maps or infographics. Skim the text quickly, and scan for any key words before reading in detail (see pages 8 and 14).

2 Use vocabulary strategies

Here are some strategies to use if you find a word or phrase you're not sure of:

- **Use context** to guess the meaning of new words (see page 108).
- **Look at word parts** (e.g., affixes) to work out what a word means (see pages 45 and 169).
- **Look for definitions** of new words within the reading passage itself.
- **Use a dictionary** if you need, but be careful to identify the correct definition (see page 39).

3 Take notes

Note-taking helps you identify the main ideas and details within a text. It also helps you stay focused while reading. Try different ways of organizing your notes, and decide on a method that best suits you (see pages 93 and 155).

4 Infer information

Not everything is stated directly within a text. Use your own knowledge, and clues in the text, to make your own inferences and "read between the lines" (see page 71).

5 Make connections

As you read, look for words that help you understand how different ideas connect. For example:

- words that show the **order of events** (see page 79)
- words that explain **cause-and-effect** relationships (see page 141)
- words that introduce **examples** (see page 164)

6 Read critically

Ask yourself questions as you read a text. For example, if the author presents a point of view, is enough supporting evidence provided? Is the evidence reliable? Does the author give a balanced argument? (see page 113)

7 Create a summary

Creating a summary is a great way to check your understanding of a text. It also makes it easier to remember the main points. You can summarize in different ways based on the type of text. For example:

- **timelines** (see page 79)
- **T-charts** (see page 108)
- **concept maps** (see page 93)
- **visual summaries** (see page 88)